Compliance-Driven DevOps: Building Audit-Ready Delivery Pipelines

Mahendar Ramidi ,
, Prudhvi Raju Mudunuri

notionpress
.com

INDIA • SINGAPORE • MALAYSIA

ISBN

Paperback 979-8-90392-525-4
Hardcase 979-8-90392-526-1

Contents

Preface

This book, ***Compliance-Driven DevOps: Building Audit-Ready Delivery Pipelines***, addresses the critical challenge organizations face today: delivering software rapidly while adhering to stringent regulatory standards. It highlights how evolving frameworks like GDPR, HIPAA, and PCI DSS have shifted compliance from being a periodic audit task to an ongoing operational necessity. Simultaneously, it shows how DevOps practices—automation, CI/CD pipelines, and cloud-native approaches—have transformed software delivery.

The book offers practical strategies to harmonize these two domains by embedding governance, security, and traceability into automated workflows. It reframes compliance not as an obstacle to innovation but as an integral feature that enhances system reliability and trustworthiness.

Targeted at technology leaders, engineers, and compliance professionals, this resource provides actionable insights for designing delivery pipelines that are inherently secure, transparent, and ready for audits by default.

This book provides the reader with some of the possible frameworks and architectures that may be employed to ensure that regulatory compliance is directly implemented in the existing DevOps processes by organizations. Among the key contributions, there are Compliance-First CI/CD Architecture, Policy-as-Code Governance Model, and Continuous Compliance Monitoring Framework. These techniques extend beyond the traditional DevOps practices of directly including governance, risk management, and security validation in automated delivery pipelines. These models provide a systematic method for the development of delivery systems that are automatically managed, policy-conformant, and can be audited, which can be translated into infrastructure as code, automatically transparent, secure, and auditable. It is the structures suggested in this book that may be particularly relevant to the organizations, the operations of which are regulated by the norms of such realms as healthcare, financial services, and governmental technologies, where the issue of constant compliance and operational accountability is one of the main aspects of concern.

The architectural frameworks and compliance automation models presented in this book were primarily developed under the leadership of Prudhvi Raju Mudunuri. His work focuses on designing enterprise infrastructure architectures that embed governance, security validation, and regulatory traceability directly into automated CI/CD pipelines. These models reflect his research and professional experience in building secure, compliant, and audit-ready delivery systems for regulated digital environments.

Mahendar Ramidi contributed to sections focused on mobile architecture and digital service design for healthcare and government platforms, complementing the broader infrastructure and compliance engineering frameworks described in this book.

The book targets technology leaders, DevOps engineers, and architects, as well as compliance professionals who need practical ways of designing highly automated delivery systems and ones that are compliant in nature. With governance and security built into the fabric of software delivery pipelines, organizations are able to leave reactive compliance efforts behind and instead design systems that are trustworthy, transparent, and ready to be subjected to regulatory scrutiny all the time.

Dedication

We dedicate this book to the engineers, architects, and compliance professionals who work tirelessly behind the scenes to build secure and reliable systems.

To our families, whose patience, encouragement, and unwavering support made this journey possible. Your belief in us provided the strength and inspiration needed to bring this work to life.

And to the global technology community striving to balance innovation with responsibility—may this book contribute to your mission of building systems that inspire trust and create lasting impact.

Acknowledgement

We would like to sincerely thank the colleagues, mentors, and industry professionals who generously shared their insights and encouragement throughout the creation of this book. Their hands-on experience in DevOps engineering, cybersecurity, and regulatory governance has been invaluable in shaping the concepts and frameworks presented here.

Our deepest gratitude also goes to the wider technology community. The shared knowledge found in conferences, research papers, and open-source projects continues to drive forward secure and compliant software delivery practices. The spirit of collective innovation within this community has greatly inspired the ideas expressed in these pages.

We are profoundly grateful to our families and friends for their steadfast support, patience, and understanding during the writing journey. Their encouragement enabled us to dedicate the time and focus needed to complete this work.

Lastly, we thank every professional committed to building secure, responsible, and audit-ready systems—your dedication to excellence fuels our motivation and inspiration.

Chapter 1

Foundations of Compliance-Driven DevOps

1.1 KEY COMPLIANCE STANDARDS AND REGULATORY FRAMEWORKS

DevSecOps compliance is vital for security and regulatory compliance. It incorporates compliance into the DevOps process, which will provide a secure and efficient development environment. Why does this matter? The compliance assists the organizations in complying with the law and safeguarding sensitive information. It protects against violations and fines.

Difficulties with compliance exist. A lot of organizations do not cope with keeping abreast of evolving rules. Ensuring that all components of the DevOps pipeline comply with the norms can be overwhelming. DevSecOps shines in this case. It offers a systematic procedure to deal with these problems.

Compliance is not something cared about in DevSecOps. It is a part of the development process itself. Such integration implies that security concerns would include all phases, including planning and implementation. The process of compliance is not a scramble but a constant struggle (Faghihi, 2025).

1.1.1 Embedding Security with DevSecOps Practices

DevSecOps revolves around security. It is embedded in the aspects of the development process. This will make security not an appendix but an essential ingredient. DevSecOps enables security to be a collective responsibility through the combination of the development, security, and operations teams. This is an endeavor aimed at enhancing the security posture of applications, and it is in line with industry standards.

It is necessary to use tools such as Control Gates, Static Application Security Testing (SAST), Dynamic Application Security Testing (DAST), and Software Composition Analysis (SCA). The devices are applied to handle security checks automatically and make sure the vulnerabilities are detected in time. These mechanisms help identify vulnerabilities early in the development lifecycle and ensure that security controls are consistently applied across the pipeline. By integrating automated security validation into cloud-native development environments, organizations can strengthen their DevSecOps practices while maintaining operational efficiency. This approach enables engineering teams to deliver software that is secure, resilient, and aligned with regulatory and enterprise governance requirements.

The following is the manner in which security is incorporated at every level:

1. **Planning:** The project defines security requirements during its initial phase to ensure that all its stakeholders understand the same.
2. **Development:** The development team uses SAST to conduct continuous security assessments of code, which enables them to identify emerging security threats.
3. **Testing:** The DAST and SCA security testing tools execute comprehensive security assessments to verify that applications meet security requirements before they go live.
4. **Deployment:** The Control Gates system enforces security regulations by permitting only verified secure code to proceed through the system.

5. **Monitoring:** The security system conducts continuous assessments to safeguard against emerging threats while maintaining required compliance standards.

The process of integrating security into DevSecOps enables organizations to fulfill their regulatory obligations while strengthening their application security framework. Organizations need to create an environment that makes security the top concern during all processes.

1.1.2 Compliance Automation in DevSecOps

DevSecOps automating the compliance process makes it easier. Continuous Compliance Automation (CCA) is an important feature as it places security checks in the development pipeline. Compliance is quicker and more efficient with this automation as fewer people are involved.

Automation tools are vital. They assist in ensuring compliance by carrying out security checks on a regular basis. This makes applications regulatory compliant and audit-ready. Errors are reduced by automating these processes, and speed increases. The result? A lean, mean security system.

Benefits of Compliance Automation:

- **Speed:** The development process achieves faster progress through quicker completion of compliance assessments.
- **Error Reduction:** The system reduces human mistakes through automated systems, which maintain uniformity in legal standards.
- **Regulatory Alignment:** The tools assist businesses in maintaining industry standards through our complete digital transformation services, which use technology to align processes and optimize their resources.

The automatic processes of automation create advantages for database compliance testing. The system secures sensitive information through its database security features, which protect data. The system guarantees secure data handling together with full compliance with legal requirements.

DevSecOps requires automated systems to create a compliance system that operates in a continuous mode. The system enables businesses to maintain compliance through its constant tracking of upcoming regulations. The method provides protection against security breaches, together with legal fines while it also improves business operations. The system makes security a fundamental requirement that exists throughout all development processes, which creates an entire development space that operates with high security standards.

What is a compliance and regulatory framework?

Compliance and regulator systems are guidelines and best practices. Such guidelines are adhered to in order to comply with regulatory standards, enhance operations, enhance security, and attain other business goals (such as becoming a publicly-traded company or selling cloud services to governmental organizations).

These frameworks do provide us with a common language that can be applied in the server room to the boardroom. These standards are capitalized on by:

- The internal auditors and other internal stakeholders to assess what controls are being carried out in their own organization.
- The external auditors to examine and certify the controls existing in an organization.
- Third parties (possible customers, investors, etc.) to identify the possible risks of collaborating with an organization.

Compliance through a regulatory framework is never a one time process. The environment you are in is never constant and the operating effectiveness of a control can disintegrate. Regular monitoring and reporting is also required, and advice given on what exactly constitutes regular monitoring is also stated in each of these frameworks.

1.1.4 DEVOPS BEST PRACTICES FOR REGULATED INDUSTRIES

1. **Establish Compliance-Driven DevOps Strategies**

   The software delivery lifecycle needs complete compliance implementation because organizations with strict regulatory requirements must follow this process. The development of DevOps strategies needs to begin with regulatory requirements because these regulations serve as fundamental requirements. The development lifecycle needs organizations to establish their policies, which will cover auditing procedures, access control systems, data residency requirements, and encryption standards. The ISO standards, including HIPAA, GDPR, and SOX, can be achieved through compliance tools that perform automated validations and compliance checks, which do not impact release timelines.

2. **Implement Infrastructure as Code (IaC)**

   The regulated environments require DevOps implementation to deliver both consistent operations and complete operational traceability. The Infrastructure as Code (IaC) system enables teams to use code for infrastructure provisioning, which results in decreased manual errors and consistent deployment processes. The system creates audit trails that help organizations meet their compliance needs. Organizations can establish secure and compliant environments in their hybrid or multi-cloud environments through the use of IaC tools such as Terraform and AWS CloudFormation.

3. **Adopt DevSecOps for Continuous Security**

   Security requirements cannot be changed because they serve as essential requirements for all regulated industries. The DevSecOps framework, which integrates security measures into DevOps processes, helps organizations find and fix security issues during the initial project development phase. This method establishes automated processes for both static code assessment, dependency verification, and compliance evaluation. Security testing tools need to be integrated throughout the CI/CD pipeline because this practice enables teams to achieve both operational efficiency and security safeguards, which form the foundation of successful DevOps automation.

4. **Enable Continuous Monitoring and Logging**

   The regulated environments require complete openness. The combination of continuous monitoring with centralized logging systems enables teams to detect problems as they happen while they trace security incidents and fulfill their audit obligations. The monitoring tools enable the detection of system performance issues, tracking of user behavior, and identification of compliance violations. The automated alerts, together with visual dashboards, enable organizations to keep track of their operations while they quickly handle security incidents.

5. **Encourage a Culture of Collaboration and Governance**

   Successful DevOps solutions require both their tools and their organizational culture, which shares responsibility with others. Development and operations teams, together with security and compliance teams, need to establish effective collaboration methods. Organizations should develop governance policies and implement role-based access controls as their primary method of establishing accountability. The organization establishes its DevOps mindset through training and communication, which emphasizes transparency, compliance, and innovation.

1.1.5 How to Achieve Compliance: Step-by-Step Guide

Implementing compliance in your organization is easier when approached systematically. Follow these steps:

1. **Understand Your Regulatory Landscape:** Identify the laws, regulations, and industry standards that apply to your market, location, and operations — such as GDPR, CCPA, HIPAA, ISO 27001, or financial reporting requirements.

2. **Assign Ownership:** Appoint a compliance lead (or team) responsible for tracking regulations, coordinating compliance activities, and ensuring accountability.
3. **Assess Requirements and Risks:** Map applicable regulations to your operations. Conduct a **Risk and Control Assessment** to pinpoint areas most vulnerable to breaches and prioritize corrective measures.
4. **Create or Update Policies:** Document policies for data handling, risk management, incident reporting, and other compliance-related processes.
5. **Develop a Compliance Strategy:** Build a roadmap detailing the controls, procedures, and timelines needed to meet compliance objectives.
6. **Train and Educate Staff:** Provide training on compliance requirements, ethical conduct, and employee responsibilities to reduce human error.
7. **Leverage Technology:** Automate documentation, reporting, and monitoring using compliance management tools. Cloud solutions are able to minimize administrative overhead, particularly when working with small teams.
8. **Monitor and Report:** Establish mechanisms that will monitor the status of compliance continuously, indicate when there are likely problems, and report them in time to the regulators.
9. **Audit and Review Regularly:** Observe compliance, identify gaps, and keep in check with the changing regulations by periodically conducting internal or external audits.

These steps are able to turn compliance into a responsive, rather than proactive, strategic part of business operations.

1.2 EVOLUTION OF DEVOPS IN REGULATED ENVIRONMENTS

The fact that the regulated sphere is developing DevOps evidences the drastic change in the manner in which organizations find the right balance between innovation and regulation. DevOps was originally employed in the less-regulated digital industries where rapidity and nimbleness were valued by automating, collaborating, and integrating continually. However, after the digitalization of industries such as finance, healthcare, telecommunication, energy, and government, the standard DevOps model has been required to be modified. The data protection, auditability, risk management, and operational resilience regulatory requirements necessitated a more formalized and compliance-aware application of DevOps. Consequently, companies began incorporating governance controls, security verification, and automated compliance directly into the development pipelines, thereby producing what is today referred to as compliance-based DevOps and DevSecOps. It is not a tradeoff between agility and control, and it is a direction of growth towards constant delivery and constant governance (Singirikonda, 2025).

1.2.1 From Waterfall Governance to Agile Delivery

Before the introduction of DevOps, the Waterfall model was largely applicable in software development within the regulated industries. The key feature of this approach was that it was linear in nature, with its extensive upfront planning and formal documentation, gates of approval, and specific stages (requirements, development, testing, and deployment). As far as Waterfall provided good governance, traceability, and audit documentation, which was important in meeting the regulations, it was also slow and hard at times, and could not be used in a dynamic business environment.

It has become a fact that organizations have begun to adopt Agile practices to have quicker response times and reduced time-to-market due to the accelerating pace of digital transformation. Agile introduced the concepts of iterative development, incremental release, and tightening contacts with stakeholders. However, Agile made no alterations to the flexibility of the development; in most instances, operational processes were not altered. The deployment, infrastructure management, and production support remained in separate operation teams, which led to bottlenecks and reintroduction of delays.

The second step in the evolution was DevOps, which unified operations and development in a single workflow relying on automation and shared responsibility. This action was to combine the agility of Agile and stability in operations. But in controlled industries, the change was to be effected very cautiously, balancing agility against governance, to be convinced that compliance problems were not put at stake.

1.2.2 Emergence of DevOps

DevOps is a type of software development methodology that integrates both development (Dev) and IT operations (Ops) with the help of automation, collaboration, and continuous delivery practices. The primary objective is to reduce the software development lifecycle and yet achieve high quality, reliability, and operational performance.

The most important ones are Continuous Integration (CI), Continuous Delivery (CD), automated testing, infrastructure as code (IaC), and continuous monitoring, which enables teams to release smaller and more frequent and consistent updates. DevOps may assist in enhancing efficiency, reducing deployment failures and enhancing the overall system resiliency through breaking down the traditional silos and enforcing a shared responsibility.

Still, early adoptions of DevOps were more of a speed centric, more automation-centric, and more culturally-centric, as compared to more formal control compliance rules that occur in highly regulated fields.

1.2.3 The Compliance Gap in Early DevOps

Despite the fact that the DevOps approach has significantly contributed to the delivery speed and collaboration, its adoption at the beginning has been a risk to the compliance of highly-regulated industries (finance, healthcare, energy, and government) of operation.

Traditional regulatory controls require a systematic approach to a change, documents of approvals, segregation of duties, an audit trail, and assessment of risks. Initial DevOps pipelines that had been designed to be fast to deploy and were constantly integrated had no embedded mechanisms of:

- Automated evidence gathering.
- Extensive audit history.
- Policy implementation controls.
- Technical control regulatory mapping.
- Institutionalized governance entry points.

The focus on quick release at times went against regulatory requirements of stability, traceability, and accountability. Organizations in other cases found more audit findings as a result of poorly written documentation on infrastructure changes, poor access controls, or no monitoring transparency.

This deviation showed that speed is not enough in regulated settings. DevOps demanded some structural improvements in order to make compliance and governance co-exist with agility.

1.2.4 Rise of DevSecOps and Continuous Compliance

Organizations began to incorporate security and governance controls into their DevOps processes because they needed to resolve compliance issues, which resulted in the development of DevSecOps and continuous compliance frameworks. DevSecOps integrates security measures throughout the software development lifecycle instead of treating security as a task for post-development work. The CI/CD pipeline uses security testing tools, which include Static Application Security Testing (SAST), Dynamic Application Security Testing (DAST), and Software Composition Analysis (SCA) to detect security weaknesses during the initial development phases. Organizations developed machine-readable policies to express their regulatory requirements, which led to the creation of Policy-as-Code in 2017. The infrastructure-as-code (IaC) framework enhances compliance because it provides version-controlled infrastructure settings that maintain detailed records for audit purposes. The organization maintains ongoing compliance through its system of continuous compliance, which it implements through:

The automated control validation.

- Instant compliance checking.
- Continuous risk assessment
- Automated audit evidence generation.

The organization will establish compliance as an ongoing validation process, which will execute automated checks during normal business activities.

1.2.5 Modern Regulated DevOps Model

The DevOps regulated model that is currently utilized is the fully grown integration of agility, security, and governance. Compliance is not seen as a hindrance by organizations, but a characteristic of design that organizations incorporate into the engineering processes.

The significant aspects of this model are:

- **Unlimited Checking and Testability:** In the monitoring system, real-time monitoring systems are used to view the performance of the infrastructure, security-related activity, and policy violations. Immutable logs and a centralized logging platform ensure audit readiness and forensic traceability.
- **Infrastructure as Code (IaC):** All infrastructures deployed are defined in versionable code repositories that are peer-reviewed, subject to auto-tests, and rollable. This ensures that change management and environment are stable and traceable.
- **Automated Compliance Controls:** CI/CD pipelines introduce controls of the regulations, such as that nonconforming code or infrastructure settings cannot be provided to production through the automated validation checks.

- **Co-location with Site Reliability Engineering (SRE):** The goals of the SRE practices are measurable reliability objectives, service levels objectives (SLO), and error budgets, such that the operational resilience is consistent with the regulatory expectations of system availability and risk tolerance.
- **Audit-Ready Pipelines:** The new pipelines can automatically collect artifacts, logs, approval records, and test results, develop structured audit evidence, and do not require any manual intervention.

DevOps in controlled environments within this developed framework is an engineering discipline that is governance-focused. It presents the optimal mix between rapidity and regulation, creativity and responsibility, automation and risk control- to realize sustainable digital change within the regulatory framework.

1.3 RISK MANAGEMENT AND CONTROL OBJECTIVES IN DEVOPS

The risk management in a modern DevOps setting should transform into something more than a periodic definition of governance, but rather something ongoing, embedded as a discipline that is a part and parcel of the software delivery lifecycle. DevOps creates unparalleled operational, automation, compliance, and resilience risks because of its speed, automation, and distributed nature, which can no longer be managed effectively using traditional control models only. Rather, companies, especially those within regulated sectors, need to establish specific control aim which connects the rate of development to the degrees of hazard, regulatory requirements, and corporate administration requirements. DevOps is changing risk management as a reactive checkpoint with automated controls, traceability mechanisms, and proactive practices of risk identification in CI/CD pipelines, and making it a systematic, measurable, and auditable capability. (Bigham, 2022).

1.3.1 Risk Management in DevOps Environments

The DevOps environment needs a governance model that provides continuous protection while tracking engineering speed against enterprise risk limits through its proactive governance system. The DevOps delivery system introduces three new elements that change how organizations assess their operational hazards because it uses fast development cycles, automatic infrastructure creation, and shared control over resources. In DevOps, risk reaches beyond its previous boundaries. The system now encompasses:

- Continuous integration and delivery systems
- Infrastructure-as-Code templates
- Cloud system setup files
- Container management frameworks
- Third-party application programming interfaces and open-source software components

The organization must assess risks almost immediately because it conducts multiple software deployments throughout each day. The unregulated access techniques used in regulated industries are as follows:

- Privileged-escalation/unauthorized access.
- Vulnerable third-party dependencies
- Poorly-configured cloud infrastructure.
- Inadequate audit trails
- Violation of data protection requirements.
- Lack of separation of duties in automated pipelines.

Best practices of successfully applying DevOps risk management are built on the following practices:

- Continuous risk identification
- Automated preventive and detection control.

- Measurable control effectiveness
- Ongoing compliance validation

The developed DevOps risk programs are beneficial to the organization as they reduce delivery time and develop the effective force of operation through their management of unexpected factors that facilitate safe, large-scale changes.

1.3.2 Shift-Left Risk Identification

The shift-left strategy is a paradigm change in terms of organizational risk recognition and risk management practices. DevOps does not view security and compliance as downstream verification activities, but rather as part of the development process.

This methodology is consistent with the contemporary secure software engineering, wherein defects and vulnerabilities are handled at the least possible level, at the time when the cost of remediation is the smallest, and the impact on the system is the lightest.

Key mechanisms include:

- During the development, Static Application Security Testing (SAST) of insecure code patterns is performed.
- Test environments, Dynamic Application Security Testing (DAST) to find runtime vulnerabilities.
- Software Composition Analysis (SCA) to detect vulnerabilities in open-source libraries
- Infrastructure-as-Code scanning to prevent configuration drift and cloud misconfigurations
- Policy-as-Codes to implement policy compliance requirements in a programmable way.

Organizations can make sure that by introducing these mechanisms in CI / CD pipelines, they will have ensured that:

- Non-compliant builds fail automatically
- Vulnerabilities are detected before production

- Developers receive immediate feedback

The shift-left approach also leads to a sense of responsibility among the developers and encourages the culture of risk ownership (risk sharing) as opposed to assigning risks to security teams at the end of the cycle.

1.3.3 Control Objectives in DevOps

Control objectives show the intended results of governance tools applied in DevOps settings. In the case of regulated sectors, such objectives are expected to be in line with enterprise risk management systems and external compliance requirements, including:

- International Organization for Standardization (ISO/ IEC 27001)

National Institute of Standards and Technology (NIST Cybersecurity Framework).

- Industry-related laws (ex, financial, healthcare, or data protection requirements)

In DevOps, the idea of control goals should be redefined to include the automation and distributed models of ownership.

The key control goals are:

Control of Change Management: Change management of both code and infrastructure must be authorized, peer-reviewed, tested, documented, and traceable. Verifiable change histories are offered by automated approval gates and version-controlled repositories.

1. **Access Control:** Introduce role-based access control (RBAC), least-privilege principles, and segregation of duties between the development, testing, and production environments.
2. **Auditability and Traceability:** Create unchanging logs throughout the repositories, pipelines, and runtime environments to enable forensic examination and regulatory audits.

3. **Vulnerability Management:** Find, rank, eliminate, and verify security vulnerabilities in applications, containers, and infrastructure elements continuously.

4. **Infrastructure Integrity:** Use Infrastructure as Code (IaC) to make system configurations repeatable and reviewable, and compliant with policy. Environmental drift is avoided by weather robotics.

5. **Compliance Evidence Automation:** Automate control evidence collection to ease regulatory audit, reduce the burden of manual record keeping, and ensure transparency.

It should have clear control objectives that will be able to assure that governance discipline is not compromised by the DevOps agility.

1.3.4 Risk Mitigation Mechanism of automation

DevOps risk mitigation is founded on automation. It reduces human error, enforces consistency of policy, and provides scalable control checking in highly distributed and complex environments.

Only automated mechanisms may have:

- Security gates based on pipelines.
- Automated mechanism of checks.
- Incremental validation of configuration.
- On-the-fly vulnerability scanning.
- Drift in infrastructure detection.

The preventive controls may automatically stop non-compliant code from advancing to production, and the detective controls detect anomalies after deployment.

Automation, however, is not the solution since it does not mitigate the risk. Overuse of tools may lead to:

- False positives and erosion of developer confidence.
- False negative because of improperly set scanning rules.

- Architectural or business-logic blind spots.

Therefore, the concept of automation should be controlled with a mechanism that incorporates:

- Risk-based prioritization
- Periodic human review
- Exception management processes.
- Executive management and reporting.

The best model is the one that combines automated enforcement and contextual risk evaluation.

1.3.5 Continuous Risk Monitoring and Feedback Loops

With DevOps, risk management is not finished upon deployment, but it proceeds into the runtime operations via ongoing monitoring and feedback measures.

Risk monitoring involves monitoring:

- Application performance anomalies
- Security events and intrusion attempts
- Policy violations
- Infrastructure configuration drift
- Service-level objective (SLO) breaches

Integration with observability platforms and Site Reliability Engineering (SRE) practices enables organizations to define measurable reliability and resilience targets.

Response twists are serious. Lessons learned from incidents, vulnerabilities, and performance failures must be reintegrated into:

- Development standards
- Pipeline validation rules
- Architecture patterns
- Control refinements

This continuous feedback cycle transforms risk management from a reactive compliance function into an adaptive engineering discipline embedded across the DevOps lifecycle.

1.4 SHARED RESPONSIBILITY BETWEEN DEVOPS AND COMPLIANCE TEAMS

DevOps transformation will not be successful in controlled settings unless the allocation of responsibility in regards to risk, controls, and compliance are redefined within the organization. In the olden days, compliance functions used to perform the role of oversight bodies, which verifies the compliance with the regulatory requirements upon the completion of the development. Devops, though, brings about continuous integration, continuous deployment, automated infrastructure provisioning and rapid release cycles which makes traditional checkpoint-based governance models non-operative.

DevOps and Compliance teams need to have a shared responsibility model in order to safely operate at scale. The model guarantees that regulatory controls are not perceived as external audit requirements, but rather as part and parcel of engineering, as inherent in the software delivery pipelines.

The shared responsibility conception under this case does not imply watered-down accountability. Instead, it establishes explicit ownership, cooperation models, and robotic implementation structures that are on pace with innovation and regulatory assurance (Nduhiu, 2025).

1.4.1 From Oversight to Embedded Governance

Under traditional IT governance model:

- Development teams build systems
- Security teams review vulnerabilities
- Compliance teams validate adherence
- Audit teams assess documentation

This linear model adds delays and, in most cases, raises problems towards the end of lifecycle.

DevOps necessitates a change to embedded governance where:

- Compliance requirements are converted to technical controls.
- Security policies are codified into pipeline validations
- Audit evidence is generated automatically
- Risk metrics are continuously monitored

Compliance is no longer a final gate. It gets incorporated as a design partner in identifying control goals and quantifiable results.

1.4.2 The definition of clear role delineation.

A fully-developed shared responsibility framework draws a very clear line between the implementation of control and control oversight.

DevOps Responsibilities

The delivery pipeline entails operationalizing controls in the delivery pipeline by DevOps teams. They are required to do the following:

- Implementing secure CI/CD workflows
- Embedding security testing (SAST, DAST, SCA)
- Configuring Infrastructure as Code (IaC) securely
- Enforcing role-based access controls (RBAC)
- Maintaining traceability of deployments
- Monitoring runtime behavior and system health
- Remediating vulnerabilities within defined SLAs

DevOps owns the execution of controls.

Compliance Responsibilities

The governance definition, validation and regulatory interpretation are done by compliance teams. They are required to do the following:

- Interpreting regulatory requirements
- Defining control objectives

- Establishing risk tolerance thresholds
- Validating control effectiveness
- Conducting risk assessments
- Ensuring audit readiness
- Reporting compliance posture to executive leadership

Compliance owns the assurance and accountability framework.

1.4.3 Control Ownership and RACI Alignment

Regulatory gaps are mainly caused by ambiguity in ownership of control. That is why, all significant DevOps controls have to be adopted in a structured RACI model (Responsible, Accountable, Consulted, Informed) in organizations.

For example:

Control Area	DevOps	Compliance
CI/CD Security Scanning	Responsible	Consulted
Access Control Policy	Responsible	Accountable
Regulatory Mapping	Consulted	Responsible
Audit Evidence Collection	Responsible (automation)	Accountable
Risk Acceptance Decisions	Consulted	Accountable

The model avoids redundancy of effort and the assumptions by who is liable to the regulatory exposure

1.4.5 Integrating Compliance into DevOps Workflows

The best shared responsibility models will include the part of the compliance in development processes in the form of automation.

Some major integration processes are:

- Policy-as-Code frameworks
- Automated control validation gates
- Compliance checks embedded in pull requests

- Continuous configuration monitoring
- Automated evidence capture from pipelines
- Immutable logging and traceability systems

By codifying compliance requirements, organizations reduce manual interpretation errors and improve consistency across environments.

This technique facilitates continuous compliance that is, control validation is conducted in real time as opposed to the annual audits.

1.4.6 Shared Accountability in Cloud Environments

The use of the clouds also adds a complication on the lines of responsibility. The customers have accountability over:

- Data classification and protection
- Identity and access management
- Encryption configuration
- Logging and monitoring
- Backup and recovery controls
- Regulatory alignment

Internally, DevOps implements these safeguards, while Compliance ensures they meet regulatory requirements and contractual obligations defined in service level agreements (SLAs).

What amounts to compliance failure is the misinterpretation of the boundaries of cloud responsibility, especially in sectors that have rigid data protection requirements.

1.4.7 Communication and Governance Forums.

Shared responsibility implies the organized communication between DevOps and Compliance teams.

Good governance mechanisms entail:

- Joint risk review committees

- Monthly compliance metric dashboards
- Incident postmortem reviews with regulatory impact assessment
- Pre-deployment risk sign-offs for high-impact changes
- Continuous control performance reporting

These forums create transparency and ensure alignment between engineering execution and regulatory strategy.

1.4.8 Cultural Alignment and Psychological Safety

Shared responsibility is a requirement that goes beyond processes and tooling to the cultural level of maturity.

DevOps teams should be empowered to:

- Raise security concerns
- Escalate potential compliance risks
- Question architectural decisions

Compliance teams must avoid positioning themselves as enforcement-only authorities. They are supposed to be as strategic partners with the ability to innovate safely instead.

The culture of trust, transparency, and shared objectives minimizes friction and enhances the results of the regulatory process.

1.4.9 Measuring Effectiveness of Shared Responsibility

Objective measures that should be used to determine the efficacy of this model include:

- Percentage of automated control validation
- Mean time to remediate vulnerabilities
- Audit findings related to DevOps processes
- Policy violation frequency
- Deployment success rate without compliance exceptions

- Evidence collection automation rate

Measurable indicators show the performance of shared responsibility.

1.4.10 Avoiding Common Pitfalls

The following are some of the challenges faced by organizations on a regular basis:

- Compliance as an after-thought.
- In-governance of over-automation.
- Lack of definition of clarity in ownership of control.
- Absence of document trailability.
- Regulatory liability on cloud providers.

These pitfalls can be resolved through formal governance structures, effective executive sponsorship and cross-functional work.

DevOps and Compliance teams need to distribute their roles as this is the case in all the regulated environments and the teams need to work together to ensure their systems achieve operational efficiency. Organizations achieve delivery speed and regulatory compliance by establishing control ownership through automated pipeline compliance integration and governance forum alignment, and their active development of collaborative organizational culture. The model creates a system that transforms compliance from a reactive checkpoint into an integrated engineering capacity that drives secure innovation and operational resilience and continuous delivery audit readiness.

1.5 BENEFITS AND CHALLENGES OF AUDIT-READY PIPELINES

The system of DevOps uses audited pipelines to achieve continuous compliance requirements that exist at all times. Organizations create their CI/CD pipelines as controlled environments that automatically implement their policies while generating documentation and tracking system activities instead of treating audits as single validation processes.

The governance system attained significant improvements through this model, yet it introduced architectural, operational, and organizational complexities that require proper management(Natarajan, 2025).

1.5.1 Benefits of Audit-Ready Pipelines

1. **Institutionalization of Continuous Compliance**

   - The process of building and testing and deploying software includes embedded compliance controls.
   - The delivery system now includes governance as an integrated system component that operates from the start.
   - The system requires organizations to enforce regulatory requirements through active monitoring instead of conducting post-implementation checks.
   - The practice of executing controls continuously helps to maintain control effectiveness throughout time.
   - Organizations transition from preparing for audits to designing their entire audit process.

   The system transforms compliance into an active business function that organizations can use at all times.

2. **Automated and Immutable Audit Evidence Generation**

   - The system records all code commits and approvals and artifact promotions and production deployments without any manual input.
   - Any changes in Infrastructure-as-Code (IaC) are also subject to version control and it is possible to follow the development.
   - All security scan results, vulnerability assessments, and policy validation results are stored in orderly storage in the system.
   - The evidence is developed by engineers in the course of their routine work, and it is not necessary to collect the evidence manually.

The system decreases three specific types of errors, which include documentation mistakes and evidence deficiencies, and post-event change history reconstruction.

The pipeline functions as an active auditing system that maintains continuous records of all activities.

3. **Enhanced Traceability and Change Accountability**

    - The system provides complete traceability from business requirement through code change to build artifact and deployment and runtime monitoring.
    - The system provides complete control ownership and approval authorities mapping.
    - Workflow automation includes validation for strong segregation of duties protection.
    - The system has enhanced root-cause analysis capabilities for incident response.

    The system enhances governance transparency which leads to greater auditor trust.

4. **Early Risk Identification and Preventive Control Enforcement**

    - Security vulnerabilities are detected during static and dynamic testing stages.
    - Policy-as-Code frameworks automatically block non-compliant configurations.
    - Infrastructure misconfigurations are identified prior to production release.
    - Automated rollback mechanisms mitigate deployment risks.
    - Preventive enforcement reduces:
    - Regulatory penalties,
    - Security exposure,
    - Remediation costs,

- Operational disruptions.

5. **Reduced Audit Disruption and Operational Burden**

- The process of preparing for audits changes from its previous system of performing audits only during specific times to a new system which allows for continuous audit preparation.
  - The evidence repositories already exist in a complete system which users can access at any time.
  - The purpose of audit investigations changes from their original function as emergency assessment periods to their new role as systems verification tests.
  - The compliance teams now spend their time on risk assessment work instead of gathering documents required for their tasks.

The organization improves its operational efficiency while decreasing the compliance burden on employees.

6. **Improved Governance Maturity and Stakeholder Trust**

- The engineering practices of the organization demonstrate connection to its regulatory obligations.
- The organization establishes trust with regulators and customers and investors through its business operations.
- The organization shows its operational control in industries that experience regulation such as finance and healthcare and telecom and public sector.
- The organization uses its third-party certification programs to support its certification and third-party assurance programs.

Audit-ready pipelines serve as official evidence showing that the organization possesses governance capabilities.

7. **Strategic Alignment Between DevOps and Compliance**

- Shared responsibility for risk management should be established through this approach.

- The process decreases conflict between engineering teams and governance teams.
- Design and architectural choices receive compliance principles through this process.
- The system enables different departments to work together by providing visible control systems.

The organization achieves its goal of long-term strength through this process.

1.5.2 Challenges of Audit-Ready Pipelines

Organizations experience significant advantages from governance systems yet face multiple hindrances which stem from their internal organizational framework and cultural characteristics.

1. **Increased Architectural and Pipeline Complexity**

    - The CI/CD workflows require additional validation gates for their extension.
    - The control checks will create bottlenecks that organizations need to optimize for their processes.
    - Organizations face challenges because they need to handle complex dependency relationships between their various tools.
    - Organizations face an increased risk of pipeline system failures when their system integrations receive inadequate design work.

    Organizations need to find the right balance between strict control measures and their ability to deploy software at high speeds.

2. **Performance Overhead and Scalability Constraints**

    - The process of security scans together with compliance validations needs computing power.
    - Build processes in extensive environments will take more time to complete.

- The organization needs to plan its infrastructure requirements for evidence storage and log retention to handle its growth needs.
- The organization needs to implement optimization methods together with specific access control measures to manage its increased deployment frequency.

3. **Over-Reliance on Automation**

    - Automated tools have the potential to produce false positive results.
    - Static policies cannot detect contextual business logic risks that exist in the system.
    - Organizations that implement excessive automation will develop complete trust in their automated tools.
    - Governance systems become less effective when organizations fail to perform regular human assessments.

    Effective risk management requires human judgment as an essential factor.

4. **Cultural Resistance and Organizational Friction**

    - Developers may perceive compliance controls as constraints.
    - The organization experiences a situation where innovation goals do not match governance requirements.
    - The organization experiences resistance to change because it implements changes throughout its transformation process.
    - The organization requires employees to develop their skills in policy-as-code and compliance software tools.

    The organization requires both leadership alignment and change management strategies for success.

5. **Toolchain Integration and Standardization Challenges**
   - DevOps ecosystems require multiple vendor solutions and different platform systems.
   - There is no established evidence format which all tools must use.
   - The process of connecting different systems will result in greater danger for operational activities.
   - The different system settings which exist in various environments will decrease the ability to control operations.
6. **Regulatory Evolution and Control Drift**
   - Regulatory requirements frequently change.
   - New cybersecurity standards emerge rapidly.
   - Policy updates must be reflected in automated rules.
   - Failure to update pipelines can create silent compliance gaps.

   Continuous review and adaptive governance models are required.
7. **Risk of Over-Gating and Reduced Innovation Velocity**
   - Excessive control layers may discourage experimentation.
   - Slow-release cycles undermine DevOps objectives.
   - Overly rigid pipelines can reduce engineering autonomy.
   - Innovation may shift to "shadow" environments outside governance frameworks.

   Maintaining proportionality in control implementation is essential.

1.5.3 Balancing Governance with Agility

The challenge of meeting the equilibrium between:

- Control assures and deployment rate.
- Human supervision and automation.
- Innovation flexibility and Standardization.
- Business competitiveness and regulatory compliance.

Compliance requirements are a regulatory obligation that can be converted by organizing the design of delivery pipelines by governance systems into a competitive advantage.

Multiple Choice Questions (MCQs)

1. **Which of the following is a primary objective of compliance standards in DevOps environments?**
   A. Increase deployment frequency
   B. Reduce developer workload
   C. Ensure legal, regulatory, and security requirements are met
   D. Eliminate manual testing
2. **Which of the following is an example of a widely recognized compliance framework?**
   A. Agile Manifesto
   B. ISO 27001
   C. GitOps
   D. Scrum Guide
3. **The evolution of DevOps in regulated environments mainly focused on:**
   A. Removing all documentation requirements
   B. Increasing separation between development and operations
   C. Integrating compliance and security into automated workflows
   D. Avoiding automation

4. **In regulated industries, DevOps pipelines must primarily ensure:**
   A. Faster UI design
   B. Automated compliance validation and traceability
   C. Reduced team collaboration
   D. Elimination of risk
5. **Risk management in DevOps is primarily concerned with:**
   A. Increasing server capacity
   B. Identifying, assessing, and mitigating security and compliance risks
   C. Improving marketing strategies
   D. Reducing code complexity only
6. **Control objectives in a DevOps environment are designed to:**
   A. Eliminate developers' decision-making authority
   B. Provide measurable safeguards to meet compliance requirements
   C. Replace governance policies
   D. Increase production outages
7. **The shared responsibility model in compliance-driven DevOps emphasizes:**
   A. Compliance is solely the auditor's responsibility
   B. DevOps teams alone manage regulatory risks
   C. Collaboration between DevOps and compliance teams
   D. Ignoring documentation to speed up delivery

8. **One major challenge in building audit-ready pipelines is:**
   A. Too much automation
   B. Lack of traceability and documentation
   C. Excessive team collaboration
   D. Overuse of version control
9. **An audit-ready pipeline typically includes:**
   A. Manual code deployment only
   B. Automated logging, monitoring, and evidence collection
   C. No security testing
   D. Untracked configuration changes
10. **A key benefit of compliance-driven DevOps is:**
   A. Delayed software releases
   B. Increased regulatory penalties
   C. Continuous compliance with reduced risk exposure
   D. Elimination of governance policies

Answers

1	2	3	4	5	6	7	8	9	10
C	B	C	B	B	B	C	B	B	C

Chapter 2

Designing Secure and Compliant CI/CD Pipelines

2.1 AUTOMATED BUILD AND TEST GOVERNANCE

DevOps environments that require compliance need companies to develop automated systems that operate their processes while providing regulatory governance, risk management, and compliance assurance. The CI/CD pipeline testing and building process serves as a vital checkpoint that assesses software quality, together with security testing and regulatory compliance initiatives and enterprise risk management activities. The creation of new code, the updating of dependencies, the changing of configuration settings, and the modification of infrastructure elements create risks that affect operational processes and compliance requirements. Automated build and test governance processes track all changes through established procedures, which maintain complete control over all development activities. Organizations with advanced capabilities integrate compliance requirements into their pipeline systems instead of treating governance as an audit, which occurs after system deployment. The CI/CD system acts as a programmable control framework that continuously checks policy compliance and produces evidence of correctness while stopping non-compliant elements from proceeding. The current model uses automation to create traceable accountability through all operational activities (Bugle, 2023).

2.1.1 Governance Embedded in Build Execution

Governance starts right when a code commit initiates the pipeline. The build process needs to impose certain rules that are a reflection of the organization's policies and also take into account the regulatory requirements. Such rules could be peer reviews that must take place, the use of branch protection tools, the signing of the commits, the checking of the contributors' identities, and the approval of the pull requests being made. A company can turn these rules into a set of instructions for the build orchestration engine, and in this way, governance becomes an activity, not paperwork.

The build system functions as a control mechanism because of the governance framework, which operates through its embedded system. The system automatically denies any attempt to make unauthorized changes through direct branch commits or unsanctioned modifications before these changes can proceed to the integration process. The system stops unreviewed code from entering shared repositories while also protecting the organization from insider threats, credential theft, and process violations. The build stage governance process guarantees that all teams will follow standardization procedures throughout their work. The coding standards of large organizations experience disruptions because of their system of operating multiple development teams. The process of automated governance establishes unified enforcement procedures that do not depend on specific disciplinary actions. The system creates a system-based environment that requires compliance from users to operate effectively. The control framework of execution control becomes defendable through the implementation of governance components during the building process. The system allows organizations to prove their change control procedures because their enforcement system operates through automated processes, which require authorized, traceable permissions for any manual changes. The technical control system of governance now operates as a demonstrable technical control that organizations can use to establish governance systems.

2.1.2 Policy Enforcement Through Automation

The compliance-driven pipeline implements governance requirements through executable logic, which industry professionals refer to as policy-as-code. Organizations create machine-readable rules to enforce compliance requirements, which they implement during their build and test processes instead of using unchanging documentation to establish compliance standards.

Policy enforcement may include:

- Minimum code coverage thresholds
- Static application security testing (SAST) enforcement
- Blocking builds containing high-severity vulnerabilities
- Dependency license validation
- Infrastructure-as-Code security checks
- Secret detection scanning
- Secure configuration validation

The procedure of policy codification allows for its execution without any discrimination against different groups. The system permits no personal interpretation or management control unless there is a documented and approved authorization. The pipeline system will automatically shut down whenever it detects a vulnerability that surpasses its established threshold. The system will stop all development activities when coverage levels fall below the required standards. The system applies deterministic rules that create complete certainty about its operational processes. Policy-as-code also enables organizations to maintain version control, which applies to their governance regulations. The system maintains governance integrity through its ability to track and review compliance logic modifications, which undergo auditing processes. The system establishes meta-governance through its capacity to control governance systems. The system uses automated policy enforcement to assist with regulatory compliance through its mapping capabilities. The pipeline controls establish a direct link to external compliance frameworks, which allows tracking of technical enforcement activities through specific regulatory requirements. This mapping process enhances audit defensibility while decreasing the amount of required evidence collection work.

2.1.3 Automated Test Governance as a Compliance Gate

The compliance-driven pipeline testing process requires testing to operate beyond its primary function of evaluating functional performance. The process now functions as an organized assessment method that measures both organizational risk tolerance levels and their compliance with regulatory requirements. The system uses automated tests as compliance validation points.

A governed test architecture typically includes:

- Unit testing for logical accuracy
- Integration testing for system interaction validation
- Security testing (SAST, DAST, container scanning)
- Performance testing for reliability thresholds
- Dependency vulnerability scanning
- Configuration compliance validation

The enterprise uses testing layers to evaluate whether a build meets its established acceptance criteria. The pipeline requires the implementation of fail-fast principles to stop work when a control threshold is reached. The automated test governance system ensures that risk identification happens at the earliest possible moment. Security and compliance checks that organizations integrate into their build cycles help them detect risks during early development stages, which results in lower remediation expenses and shorter production periods.

Governance procedures for testing create testing processes that produce consistent testing outcomes. The testing process that uses manual testing methods will provide different testing outcomes. The automated tool enforces rules through its automation, which ensures all builds receive identical testing procedures, thus development teams maintain their standard testing methods.

Regulatory agencies require automated test governance to provide all essential evidence that organizations need to operate their businesses. Test execution logs, together with scan reports, coverage summaries, and remediation timelines, provide compliance documentation. The documentation proves that organizations must enforce their regulatory requirements through systematic enforcement, which operates as their standard procedure.

2.1.4 Segregation of Duties and Role-Based Controls

Regulatory frameworks require organizations to implement duty separation as a method to stop power concentration and decrease fraud possibilities. The CI/CD environment requires organizations to implement this principle through technical methods. Automated build governance system uses role-based access control (RBAC) to manage access across multiple components, which include source repositories, build systems, artifact repositories, and deployment platforms. Developers are permitted to commit code, but they are not allowed to approve their own modifications. Security teams have the authority to establish vulnerability thresholds, but they do not have permission to change production artifacts. Release managers have the authority to approve deployments, but they do not have the ability to change source code.

The system ensures delivery operations follow proper processes by using material delivery restrictions, which stop one person from managing the entire process. The system maintains process separation through its automated approval gates, which serve as a second line of defense against unauthorized access. The system provides an example through its automated approval process, which evaluates multiple approval gates before reaching a final decision:

- Pull requests require Independent review
- Security findings require documented remediation or risk acceptance
- Production deployment requires multi-party approval

The controls decrease insider threat danger while establishing monitoring systems that track responsibility throughout the entire process. The system records all actions, which include approval, override, and configuration change, with their respective user identities. Automatic segregation implementation establishes a system that maintains its operations without interruption. Operational demands cause a gradual decline in manual enforcement capabilities. The system maintains ongoing security through RBAC enforcement, which operates without interruption during rapid software development processes.

2.1.5. Artifact Integrity and Traceability

The governed build process should create an artifact that meets three requirements: immutable state, unique versioning, and complete traceability. The compliance claims do not hold when the artifact integrity is nonexistent.

Automated governance applies:

- Immutable artifact storage
- Unique version tagging
- Cryptographic checksum generation
- Controlled artifact repository access
- Promotion-based deployment models

The production artifact must match the tested and approved version exactly. Any change in the system will destroy traceability and introduce new security threats. As such, build-once systems that are deploy-many are used in the mature pipelines where artifacts are transported across various environments without being rebuilt.

Traceability associates every artifact with:

- Source commit identifiers
- Author identity
- Test execution results
- Security scan reports

- Approval history
- Deployment timestamps

The chain of custody system provides complete tracking of all movements. The forensic traceability system permits two-hour production breakdowns to be resolved through exact build tracing, which requires only two minutes. The software integrity control system shows complete control because all aspects of the system are visible to users. Supply chain security needs artifact governance because external sources create more serious risks than internal teams. The system gains better protection against injection and substitution attacks because artifact immutability prevents all changes to its content.

2.1.6 Evidence Generation and Audit Readiness

A compliance-ready pipeline continuously generates structured evidence as a byproduct of execution. Every build must produce tamper-resistant logs capturing:

- Trigger source
- User identity
- Commit identifiers
- Build configuration
- Test results
- Security scan findings
- Approval events
- Deployment status

The organization needs to store these records at a central location that must follow specific retention methods that comply with all regulatory requirements. The system uses automated retention enforcement to stop data from being deleted before its scheduled time while maintaining access to data during audit periods. The organization produces continuous evidence, which removes the need for traditional audit processes that require staff members to search for evidence at designated times. The organization can access its entire historical record of activities through its pipeline system, which provides authenticatable records that contain time stamps and structured data. The organization must protect its evidence integrity. The system must have full access control features, which involve permanent record storage and real-time monitoring of any unauthorized access to the system. Having controlled logs improves confidence in the audit since it offers a direct control measure on the management of logs. The process of evidence generation becomes part of operational activities, which enables organizations to shift from handling audits in reaction to their preparedness for upcoming audits.

2.1.7 Risk Management and Continuous Control Validation

The risk landscape of compliance requirements changes because organizations must adapt to new situations. The automated build governance system requires the development of control validation procedures, which need continuous testing. Dependency ecosystems undergo rapid changes throughout time. A component that was secure at first will eventually be discovered as vulnerable. The system requires automatic pipelines to conduct periodic dependency rescans, which apply to all software releases. The monitoring process needs to track build environment configuration changes because these changes can create security weaknesses.

Continuous validation mechanisms include:

- Scheduled re-scanning of artifacts
- Monitoring for pipeline configuration changes
- Administrative privilege audits
- Alerting on unauthorized modifications
- Version-controlled pipeline definitions

The pipeline configuration needs to be treated as code which requires formal assessment during its implementation. The unauthorized changes to governance rules will lead to hidden faults that make the enforcement process impossible to execute. The control framework needs protection through meta-controls which should monitor its operations. The governance system remains operational because its multiple validation processes maintain its functions. The organization implements controls which undergo ongoing testing to determine their operational success. The automated build and test governance system unites three essential elements, which include engineering standards, regulatory requirements, and operational responsibility. Organizations achieve operational flexibility while maintaining compliance through the implementation of mandatory controls that work with their CI/CD pipelines. The organization controls every build process through established procedures that use specific rules. The organization uses tests as official compliance assessment points. Every artifact exists as an unchangeable, observable object that moves through a visible process of custody handling. The model changes automation in highly regulated digital environments from a tool for faster productivity to a framework that establishes organizational trust. Governance becomes a built-in process that software delivery teams use to create continuous, measurable, and defendable software delivery operations.

2.2 COMPLIANCE-FIRST PIPELINE ARCHITECTURE

Digital enterprises use modern CI/CD pipelines because they need more than automated delivery systems to handle their code delivery needs. The software creation process uses these systems to design and build software while testing and distributing it to users. A compliance-first pipeline architecture establishes delivery system standards because it requires stakeholders to implement regulatory requirements and security controls and risk management practices and audit mechanisms directly into their system design. The organizations create their pipelines with built-in security features because they want to prevent security problems from happening. The architectural design of the system enables organizations to maintain their accountability while creating new solutions which comply with existing rules and business requirements (Timar, 2026).

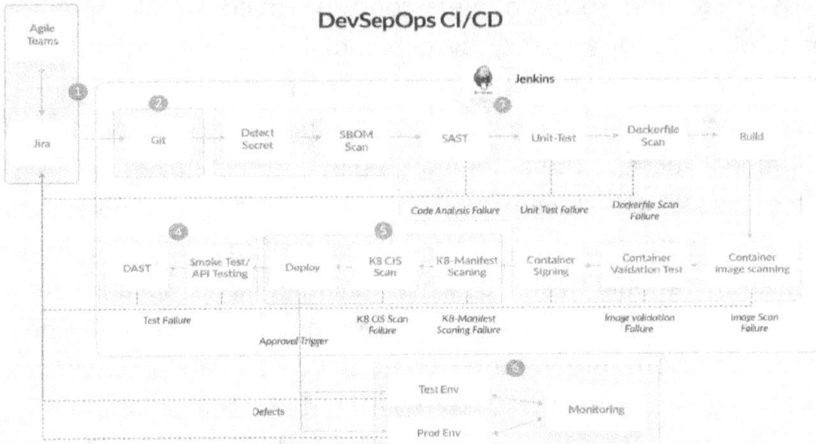

Figure 3.1: DevOps CI/CD Diagram

Figure 1 illustrates a compliance-first CI/CD pipeline architecture in which security validation, policy enforcement, and compliance controls are integrated directly into the automated delivery workflow. This architecture enables organizations to maintain continuous governance and audit readiness while supporting rapid and reliable software delivery.

- **CI/CD Pipeline for Web Applications**

  Web application CI/CD pipeline is the process of building, testing and deploying web based software systems that is automated. When the developers check code to a version control repository, the pipeline automatically triggers the build processes, runs unit and integration tests, conducts security and dependency scans and packages the application to be deployed. Staging environments are then used to promote successful builds before they are sent to the production servers or cloud platforms. This software-based workflow enhances reliability of release, minimizes the impact of human error, and provides organizations a chance to release updates to web applications faster without compromising the quality and security assurance.

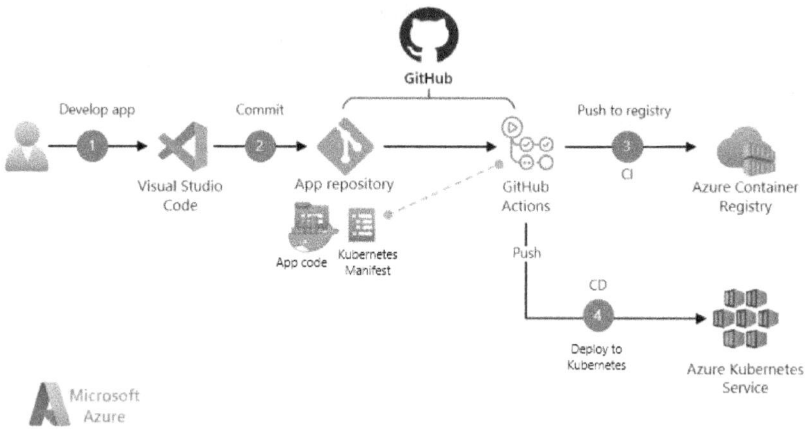

Figure 3.2: CI/CD Pipeline for Web Applications

Figure 2.3 illustrates a CI/CD pipeline used for web applications where source code commits trigger automated build, testing, artifact creation, and deployment processes across staging and production environments.

- **CI/CD Pipeline for Mobile Applications**

  A mobile application CI/CD pipeline builds upon the standard DevOps practices to add other phases needed to build a mobile platform. Once developers have written code, the pipeline will run automated Android or iOS mobile platform builds after which unit testing, UI testing via emulators or real hardware, as well as security testing is run. This pipeline would subsequently produce signed application packages and will package it to be distributed by the app stores or enterprise deployment systems. Mobile CI/CD pipelines are used to build, test, and distribute applications by automation to assist development teams to be able to keep the quality of applications and hasten the release cycle of mobile software updates.

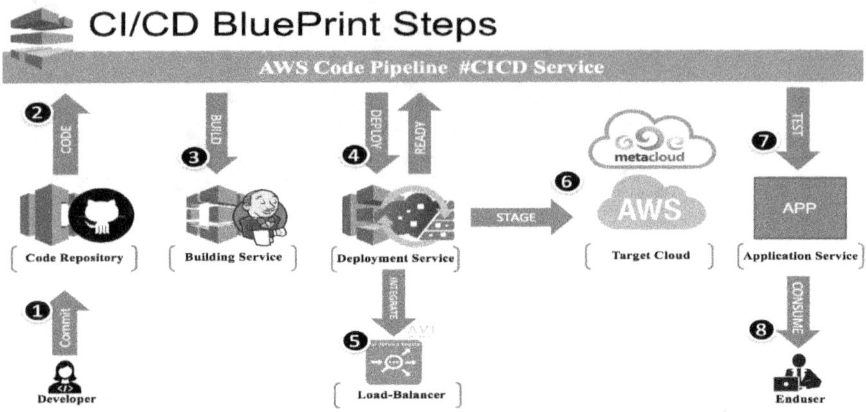

Figure 3.3: CI/CD Pipeline Architecture for Mobile Applications

Figure 2.4 illustrates a CI/CD pipeline for mobile applications where automated build systems compile Android or iOS applications, execute testing workflows, package application binaries, and distribute validated builds to testing platforms and application stores.

2.2.1 Architectural Separation of Environments

A compliance-first pipeline architecture begins with strict logical and operational separation between all four operational environments development testing staging and production. The identification of access controls and configuration baselines and promotion pathways must be established for each operational environment. Developers can deploy applications in development environments but they need to complete validation processes before they can deploy their work to staging or production. The system creates a secure environment that prevents unauthorized users from making changes that would violate quality standards and compliance requirements. The organization of environments into separate zones creates an additional layer of protection that safeguards confidential information found in production systems. Testing environments should use sanitized or synthetic datasets, which must comply with data protection regulations. Organizations must maintain dedicated production credentials which should never be used in any lower environments. The system achieves architectural separation through the use of separate infrastructure layers, which require distinct cloud accounts and subscription models and controlled access deployment credentials. The system achieves compliance through architectural design which embeds regulatory requirements into its core functions instead of treating them as separate procedures that should be implemented later.

2.2.2 Policy-as-Code as a Foundational Layer

Compliance-first architectures use executable logic to implement their security policies through coded policy rules. Organizations transform their compliance needs into machine-readable policies for direct use in pipeline workflows instead of documenting their rules through human-enforced manual systems.

These policies may enforce:

- Mandatory security scanning before artifact promotion
- Prohibition of deployments with critical vulnerabilities
- Infrastructure configuration validation
- Approved dependency usage
- Mandatory code review completion
- Regulatory tagging of builds

The CI/CD systems use their embedded policy engines to conduct real-time evaluation of builds. The pipeline system stops its development process whenever a build fails to meet compliance requirements. The system examines existing policies that provide organizational guidance to create binding enforcement mechanisms. Through policy-as-code implementation, organizations achieve scalable governance systems that allow them to integrate new regulatory requirements into their pipeline operations without needing complete system redesigns.

2.2.3 Immutable Artifact Promotion Model

The main principle that guides compliance-first architecture requires systems to maintain their original state. The build artifact must remain unchanged after it has successfully completed all validation tests until it reaches its final installation site. The exact artifact tested during staging must match the artifact that gets used in production. The system achieves its goals through the use of centralized artifact repositories combined with cryptographic hashing, version tagging, and controlled promotion mechanisms. The system uses a verified artifact that moves through controlled pathways instead of building new code for each environment. Immutability prevents three types of security risks, which include configuration drift, unauthorized changes, and untraceable modifications. The system establishes an unbroken record of all activities from commit to deployment, which makes it easier to protect audit information. The system requires all its components to maintain separation between build systems and deployment systems, while only authorized personnel should have permission to grant promotion rights.

2.2.4 Integrated Security Validation Layers

Security cannot operate as an external scanning function. In a compliance-first pipeline architecture, security validation layers are embedded at multiple stages of the CI/CD workflow.

These include:

- Static application security testing during build
- Dependency vulnerability scanning
- Infrastructure-as-code security validation
- Container image scanning
- Secrets detection
- Dynamic testing in controlled environments

Validation layers function as access points that require specific thresholds to determine acceptable risk boundaries. The system should automatically reject any build that exceeds established risk limits. The layered security model enables organizations to detect security vulnerabilities at an early stage, which helps them to decrease their remediation expenses while blocking unsafe code from being deployed. The system shows active risk management practices that security assessment organizations can observe during their examination of compliance with regulations.

2.2.5 Segregation of Duties Embedded in Pipeline Roles

Regulatory frameworks consistently emphasize segregation of duties (SoD). In a compliance-first architecture, SoD is enforced through structured role-based access control within pipeline platforms.

Architectural enforcement includes:

- Developers cannot approve their own merges
- Release approvals require independent authorization
- Security teams define scanning thresholds but cannot alter source code
- Production deployment rights are restricted to designated roles

These controls must be technically enforced through identity and access management systems integrated with the CI/CD platform.

By embedding SoD into the architecture, organizations eliminate reliance on informal agreements and reduce insider risk.

2.2.6 Comprehensive Logging and Evidence Retention

To be audit-ready, there must be full visibility on the operations of the pipeline. A compliance-first architecture requires that all the activities in the pipeline be centrally logged, such as:

- Commit metadata
- Build triggers
- Test results
- Security scan outputs
- Approval records
- Deployment timestamps
- User identities

Logs must be tamper-resistant and retained according to regulatory retention requirements.

In architecture, this normally includes integration with secure logging systems or security information and event management systems. The logs are to be searchable, exportable, and not editable.

Constant creation of evidence turns compliance into a scramble that never ends, but is an operating condition.

2.2.7 Risk-Based Deployment Gating

Changes are not equally dangerous. Compliance-first structures have risk-based gating systems, which modify the approval conditions depending on the classification of changes. Changes are not equally dangerous. Compliance-first structures have risk-based gating systems, which modify the approval conditions depending on the classification of changes.

For example:

- Minor documentation updates may require automated validation only.
- Feature releases may require peer review and security approval.
- This may involve infrastructure changes that may need extra configuration checks and risk analysis.

The pipeline has risk scoring mechanisms to enable organizations to balance scoring and control. There is increased scrutiny of high-risk deployments, and low-risk changes are run smoothly through the pipeline.

This dynamic gating methodology matches the intensity of governance and operational risk.

2.2.8 Infrastructure-as-Code Governance

Declarative templates are common in the deployment of infrastructure in modern pipelines. Compliance-first architecture brings governance to infrastructure-as-code (IaC).

Misconfigurations that should be scanned in IaC:

- Open network ports
- Excessive privileges
- Unencrypted storage
- Non-compliant resource configurations

Policy validation ensures that infrastructure deployments align with organizational security standards.

The organizations enforce code-level rules of governance over infrastructure to avoid violations of the compliance criteria even prior to infrastructure becoming available.

2.2.9 Managed Interaction with the External Systems

Essentially, a CI/CD pipeline integrates components of a wide variety of systems, including version control systems, artifact repositories, cloud providers, identity providers, and monitoring systems. A CI/CD pipeline would most likely not be a perfectly autonomous system. Besides, a first architecture, which is also known as a compliance architecture, must have not only a secure API integration but also encrypted communication channels, token management policies, and restricted service account permissions. The majority of the uncontrolled integration situations can be regarded as ports of entry by the attackers. The system is requesting a review of its architectural design, particularly the points of interaction to make sure that the compliance is maintained not only in one system but also in all systems.

2.2.10 Continuous Monitoring and Drift Detection

Compliance is not static. Changes in configuration, unauthorized permission modifications, and the shifting regulatory demands can compromise the already compliant systems.

A compliance-oriented architecture involves a constant monitoring system to identify: Pipeline configuration changes

- Disabled security gates

- Unauthorized privilege escalation
- Artifact inconsistencies
- Environment misalignments

Automated alerts and periodic compliance reviews ensure that governance remains active over time.

Drift detection enhances architectural resilience in the long run.

2.2.11 Documentation and Change Management Integration

All modifications to the pipeline that involve additional stages, change in policies as well as alterations in deployment levels must be fully documented and must contain all the modifications. The system architectural design is connected to the change management systems to ensure the development of the pipeline is controlled by controlled processes. The system also ensures compliance standards are maintained in its structure that does not allow any unauthorized changes and allows full visibility in the form of audit.

The compliance-first pipeline system conveys residential data via instituted processes of delivery that demand security and compliance of regulation to be operational. Delivery environments create by organizations ensure the performance of the organization operationally by control security systems that organizations can check and increase. Sustainable speed operates in a manner that does not exceed the set limits of operation. Defensible innovation is the product of setting up traceable systems. The architectural field contributes to the fundamental basis of providing secure software delivery in regulated digital environments.

2.3 PIPELINE SECURITY THREATS AND MITIGATION STRATEGIES

The CI/CD pipeline in compliance-focused DevOps environments operates as a vital operational asset which functions as an automated system for businesses. The increasing speed at which organizations deliver software has led attackers to focus on pipeline systems as their primary target for executing malicious attacks which include code injection and artifact theft and secret exfiltration and release process disruption. A pipeline breach will lead to compliance violations which will damage customer confidence and create enterprise-wide operational hazards. Organizations must establish pipeline security as their primary design element which protects their systems against potential threats. The process of identifying specific pipeline threats requires organizations to develop protection systems which they need to implement throughout their pipeline operations for effective performance and legal compliance(Heusser, 2024).

2.3.1 Source Code and Repository Compromise

The software supply chain starts with source control systems as its initial component. The main security threats come from unauthorized access to repositories and malicious code commits and branch manipulation and credential theft. Attackers attempt to insert backdoors into trusted codebases while exploiting weak branch protection policies to add untested code. Strong identity governance serves as the first step for all organizations that want to achieve security protection. The system mandates that all code modifications must obtain verification through multi-factor authentication and signed commits and protected branches and peer review requirements. Role-based access control (RBAC) needs to allow option of limited write access to only particular users that have been given the green light to access. Constant monitoring of repository activity, comprising of identifying uncharacteristic commit scenarios, and unearthed privilege escalation attacks, serves companies to detect potential threats at an early life stage. The controls help organizations to prevent their delivery lifecycle to suffer initial security breaches in the process of which they use the controls to trace who has changed what system.

2.3.2 Pipeline Configuration Tampering

CI/CD pipelines are programmable systems that individuals define by applying their configuration files along with automation scripts. To undermine compliance controls, an attacker can alter the functioning of the pipeline to stop security scans as they modify deployment targets and avoid approval criteria. The answer involves organizations taking pipeline definitions as code that must undergo version control and code review. Infrastructure-as-Code (IaC) and pipeline configuration files must be placed in secured repositories, and must undergo compulsory review processes. Strict access controls should be defined on orchestration platforms of pipeline access in organizations that should be audited on a regular basis. Each and every configuration change must trigger three response processes that comprise of logging and alerting and potential secondary approval processes. Constant validation of configuration integrity (via checksums or automated drift-detection) is a crucial requirement to make sure that governance logic is not modified by unauthorized individuals.

2.3.3 Dependency and Supply Chain Attacks

The existing software development model demands that the developers make use of libraries and container images and external packages that are developed by different firms. Dependencies employed by developers in their projects may generate the deficiencies in security and deploy malicious software and pose issues with adherence to the licensing policies. The attackers that engage in supply chain attacks exploit the hacked open-source software components and forged software packages to infiltrate the secured build environments. The solution to this problem involves implementing three main components which include automated scanning of dependencies and integration of vulnerability management systems and software composition analysis (SCA) tools. The build system should implement rules which prevent the creation of new builds that contain either critical security flaws or unauthorized software licenses. Organizations can decrease their risk of public repository attacks by using secure artifact repositories and their own internal package proxy systems. The development process of building software once and deploying it multiple times together with keeping track of verified artifact origins creates stronger protection for supply chain systems. The process of continuously checking dependencies after the deployment phase enables organizations to quickly identify new security vulnerabilities which they can then resolve.

2.3.4 Secrets Exposure and Credential Leakage

Pipelines require access to sensitive credentials and API keys and certificates and cloud authentication tokens. The security of secret materials is at risk because of improper handling, which lets actual content become exposed through logs and configuration files and compromised build agents. The organization needs to implement secret management systems that operate from a centralized location and connect with their pipeline operations. The secret information must not be included as permanent code in source files and it must not be kept as unencrypted rules in configuration files. The system needs to implement runtime secret injection with automatic secret changes that occur at specified times. The organization needs to establish secret record access restrictions, which require both personnel security clearance and system access records to monitor safe handling of sensitive information. The organization needs to implement automated secret detection tools, which will enable them to scan their repositories for unauthorized access to secret information.

2.3.5 Compromised Build Agents and Execution Environments

The system grants execution rights to build agents who carry out their work by executing pipeline tasks. The system enables attackers to manipulate system elements and steal confidential information and introduce destructive software into their build operations. The solution requires building secure build environments that use either container-based systems or temporary execution environments. The use of temporary build agents that function as disposable resources creates challenges for attackers who want to establish long-term presence. The network segmentation system also allows the agents to only connect to necessary communication points that they need in their operations. Build infrastructure is regularly patched and security improved that safeguards execution environments against security attacks. Two security checks, including checksum verification of generated artifacts and restriction of outbound network access during the build operation are used by the integrity validation system to guard against unauthorized data modification and theft of information.

2.3.6 Artifact Manipulation and Integrity Breach

The artifact repository is the ultimate result of the construction process. By overcoming the existing security measures, an attacker can either replace or modify the artifacts that have been stored so that he/she can inject malicious codes into production systems. . The organization protects its systems through three mitigation strategies which include enforcing artifact repository immutability and signing build outputs with cryptographic keys and using checksum verification for deployment. The organization must control access to artifact storage which should be divided into different roles. Promotion workflows should move artifacts between environments without rebuilding them, preserving integrity and traceability. The system uses audit logs to track all artifact uploads and downloads and promotions which provides complete traceability throughout the delivery process. The two systems together with digital signatures create a system that allows people to prove the custody of items.

2.3.7 Insider Threats and Privilege Escalation

The organization faces threats that come from both internal and external sources. Insiders who possess excessive access rights tend to violate security measures by either maliciously or accidentally making system changes. Security measures start when organizations implement strict controls that require users to have only essential access rights. One person should not have the ability to manage every aspect of the pipeline development process. Authority distribution decreases because organizations require staff members to receive mandatory approvals and conduct scheduled access assessments. Privileged access management systems are used by organizations to monitor and restrict the users with greater access privileges. Companies utilize full-fledged administrative action logs to monitor the use of privileges that helps them to enforce security and adherence. Tracking user activities assists organizations to uncover malicious activities that involve users who install software during odd hours and those who modify system configuration in unusual manners.

2.3.8 Logging, Monitoring, and Alerting Failures

The system displays hidden places that should be observed since there is no provision of monitoring features. The security breaches are invisible when malicious activities occur but the full logging records are unable to record all the activities. The process must have centralized logging systems that must accumulate and archive the entire contents of all the build, test, and deployment activities. This system must have permanent logs that should not be deleted or altered by any unauthorized personnel. The organization needs real-time alert systems which will identify security scan failures and abnormal pipeline activities and multiple configuration changes. Security controls need continuous monitoring to confirm their operational status and their protection against ongoing threats. The organization needs to perform regular logging validation tests because this process prevents unnoticed deterioration of security control measures.

2.3.9 Denial-of-Service and Availability Risks

CI/CD pipelines represent vital components for operational success. Attackers will try to disrupt build systems through various methods which include denial-of-service attacks and resource exhaustion and infrastructure sabotage thus preventing software delivery while disrupting business operations. The organization uses three primary strategies to prevent security threats which include building a redundant infrastructure system and implementing autoscaling capabilities and using rate-limiting security measures. High-availability pipeline architectures enable organizations to prevent their systems from experiencing operational downtime through a single failure point. Backup configurations and disaster recovery planning ensure rapid restoration of service in the event of disruption. Organizations must protect pipeline must protection through operational methods because their need for uptime and continuous operation of their systems establishes compliance requirements.

2.3.10 Continuous Security Validation and Threat Modeling

Any threat landscape is changed through rapid transformation. In order to protect their assets, organizations need to have more than just static mitigation strategies when they are operating in environments that are constantly changing. In order to secure their pipelines, companies must perform continuous threat modeling along with control validation procedures.

Organizations ought to regularly review their pipeline infrastructure in order to check how well it is protected against the latest emerging threats. Doing red, team exercises combined with penetration testing of CI/CD systems and security assessments of pipeline updates continuously validate security controls. Security testing fixes the security loopholes by its integration into the pipeline process, including the automatic run of security regression tests.

It is a must for organizations to change their governance systems if they want to keep up with the increasing complexity of their delivery processes.

Pipeline security threats combine operational risk with supply chain vulnerability and insider threat protection and regulatory liability. The DevOps compliance framework requires organizations to use security measures which go beyond single security tools and defensive response methods. Security needs to be part of system design throughout the entire CI/CD process which begins at source commit and ends at artifact deployment. Organizations establish durable delivery systems through their security practices which include multiple protective measures and restricted access rights and integrity testing and ongoing system activity monitoring. Through these actions they safeguard their software supply chain and maintain their compliance reputation and the confidence of their operational networks.

2.4 ARTIFACT INTEGRITY AND VERSION TRACEABILITY

The entire software delivery process in compliance-driven DevOps environments depends on the trustworthy nature of all its produced software artifacts which serve as its fundamental proof of success. Any organizational intention is demonstrated through an artifact which exists as a compiled binary or container image or package file or infrastructure template. The system control validation process fails when organizations cannot establish system integrity or demonstrate compliance through system monitoring. The system requires three core elements which include operational trust, regulatory confidence and security assurance to confirm the deployed system matches all built components and testing results and approved elements and authorized parts. The CI/CD pipelines which are ready for auditing purposes depend on two main components which include artifact integrity and version traceability. The system transforms delivery outputs into entities which maintain permanent records and proof through a secured system that protects all evidence (Hollowell, 2023).

2.4.1 Defining Artifact Integrity in CI/CD Contexts

The term artifact integrity assures that existing build output remains unchanged since its initial creation because both intentional and unintentional alterations to the output have been prevented. Modern DevOps systems allow artifacts to travel through various operational environments and storage systems and automated systems until they reach their final production state. Each transition presents a potential opportunity for tampering, substitution, or corruption. Organizations need to implement immutable control systems to maintain their system integrity. The system requires that users create a new version whenever they want to change an existing artifact. The system requires that users create a new version whenever they want to change an existing artifact. The system requires that users create a new version whenever they want to change an existing artifact. The system requires that users create a new version whenever they want to change an existing artifact. The system requires that users create a new version whenever they want to change an existing artifact. The system requires that users create a new version whenever they want to change an existing artifact. The system requires that users create a new version whenever they want to change an existing artifact. The system requires that users create a new version whenever they want to change an existing artifact. The system requires that users create a new version whenever they want to change an existing artifact. The system requires that users create a new version whenever they want to change an existing artifact. The system requires that users create a new version whenever they want to change an existing artifact.

The system requires that users create a new version whenever they want to change an existing artifact.The system requires that users create a new version whenever they want to change an existing artifact. The system requires that users create a new version whenever they want to change an existing artifact. The system requires that users create a new version whenever they want to change an existing artifact. The system needs to establish a new version whenever users want to change existing artifacts. The system needs to establish a new version whenever users want to change existing artifacts. The cryptographic hashing system enables the confirmation process which checks whether artifacts have maintained their complete original state. The system generates unique checksums during the build process which are then saved with the metadata of each artifact. The hashes stored in the system can be used to verify system integrity during deployment because they enable detection of any changes that occurred since the last secure state. The deployment process will automatically stop whenever the system identifies any discrepancies. Integrity exists as a measurable state because it depends on technical parameters which developers use to design their pipeline system.

2.4.2 Immutable Artifact Repositories and Controlled Storage

The function of artifact repositories is to provide secure storage locations for all build output materials. The absence of proper governance procedures creates security risks which can affect repository operations. The system becomes insecure because users can either overwrite existing artifacts or delete all previous versions or they can access all content without restrictions. Compliance-driven pipelines enforce immutability within artifact repositories. The system locks all uploaded artifacts so users cannot make any changes to them. Production and development environments have one and the same artifact used in the process of moving between the two. Access control is also of critical importance. Role-based access controls should be implemented in the system to decide which users can be authorized to have artifact upload download promotion and deletion activities. The system provides that all administrative functions must have express authorization prior to implementation and the procedure must produce audit documentation.

Organizations use repository access restrictions to stop unauthorized users from replacing or changing deployment packages. Retention policies need to follow all required regulatory standards. Organizations have to maintain historical artifacts for specific time frames which allows them to conduct forensic investigations and verify compliance when needed.

2.4.3 Versioning Strategies and Semantic Traceability

Versioning functions as an identification system which tracks all modifications and historical development of document content. The deployment of effective versioning systems enables organizations to track their active software components from the time of deployment until they reach their original source code and configuration and dependency information. Semantic versioning frameworks deliver structured version numbers which indicate how software changes through major and minor and patch updates. The requirements of compliance-driven environments necessitate that versioning systems need to establish unique identifiers which connect directly to specific source commits while preserving semantic versioning elements.

Each artifact version should map to:

- A specific source control commit hash
- Associated pull request or change request ID
- Build execution identifier
- Test and security scan results
- Approval and release authorization records

The fully integrated connection network allows for accurate tracking of the deployed artifacts back to their original sources. Version numbers evolve from being mere identifiers to becoming elements of the case through traceability. When auditors require evidence of change management control, organizations have to provide proof of deployment and show that their change management process is supported by their version control system. The feat can be done through well, organized version traceability.

2.4.4 Chain of Custody Across the Delivery Lifecycle

Chain of custody is the notion that is traditionally related to legal evidence management; it is directly relevant to the artifact management. All the transformations need to be recorded and regulated all the way the code is committed to the time the software runs in production.

A compliant pipeline establishes a continuous, traceable record of artifact movement:

- Source commit creation
- Build initiation and artifact generation
- Automated testing and validation
- Artifact repository storage
- Environment promotion
- Production deployment

The process needs to document who started each action, together with the time it happened and the permission that allowed it to take place. The established framework gives complete clarity about the origin of the artifact through its documented path of development. Organizations need to maintain complete records of their deployed artifacts because production incidents require organizations to trace back all deployment activities. Chain-of-custody documentation enables forensic investigators to work more efficiently while providing stronger legal protection for regulated industries.

2.4.5 Digital Signing and Provenance Verification

Digital signatures provide proof that an artifact originated from a secure build system which has remained unchanged since the authentication process. Build systems in complex compliance environments start to create digital signatures for their generated artifacts. The system requires signature verification to proceed with execution in restricted environments. The system uses two verification methods to block unauthorized materials from entering the production process. Provenance frameworks enhance traceability because they maintain records of build environments and dependency sources and execution contexts. The provenance records demonstrate that artifacts were created within secure environments which did not use materials from unsafe systems. Digital signing and provenance verification together create trust points that secure the software supply chain.

2.4.6 Build-Once, Deploy-Many Model

The most critical rule that preserves the integrity of the artifacts is the build-once deploy-many approach. The fact that artifacts are made by hand on an individual environment basis leads to unforeseen results that complicate change tracking. The dissimilarity in behavior of systems is brought about by varying environment settings and varying dependency versions as well as dissimilar runtime conditions. Organizations ensure system consistency by their artifact construction process by building an artifact once and then transferring it to the development, testing and production processes without modifications. The tested binary that passes the test of security as well as performance is the one that is finally implemented in production. The model reduces the chances of particular environmental changes even as it enhances on compliance reporting. All the validation results are shown in the system, which is said to be directly related to deployed artifacts, which avoids any uncertainty that may occur due to the final moment changes in the system or unsanctioned changes.

2.4.7 Traceability Across Infrastructure and Configuration

The traceability of artifacts cannot be restricted to application binaries only but also include infrastructure and configuration elements. As templates of code and container orchestration manifestation with configuration files, infrastructure is the fundamentals of the operation of the systems in the modern DevOps landscape. The versioning and immutability in addition to the designing and tracking features are all required in all the system components. The infrastructure templates will be supposed to be compatible with the specific application versions. In addition to this, organizations must maintain a highly detailed record of configuration changes in an equivalent level of detail that they maintain in tracking code changes. The entire tracking system enables the operation environments to receive the precise environmental restoration. Portraying the given code of application developed as well as the particular infrastructure and arrangement deployed, organizations can show their adherence to regulatory investigations as well as investigations of incidents.

2.4.8 Audit Evidence and Compliance Alignment

The regulatory requirements regarding change management, configuration control, and system integrity have a direct relationship with artifact integrity and version traceability. In general, compliance frameworks usually require:

- Evidence of controlled change processes
- Assurance of system integrity
- Documentation of deployment approvals
- Retention of historical versions

By embedding traceability within pipeline automation, organizations generate continuous evidence rather than retrospective documentation. The work on audit preparation is replaced by the collection of data in a systematic form. In addition, traceability enhances transparency of risk reporting and good governance. Deployment histories, timelines of vulnerability exposure and remediation actions can be consolidated and viewed by the executive stakeholders. This correspondence between the technical traceability and the governance reporting leads to increased visibility of enterprise-wide risk.

2.4.9 Continuous Validation and Integrity Monitoring

Artifact integrity validation involves numerous checks that are performed over the entire lifecycle of the project. The system scans all stored artifacts to ensure that they are completely safe and secure to any alteration. The system employs three methods that involve checksum verification, repository integrity scanning and access pattern to detect security threats in its early stages. Every administrative operation that affects repositories of artifacts must be documented and analyzed by the authorized personnel. The system will raise an alert whenever a user tries to delete, overwrite or alter artifacts stored in the system by means of alerts that will also compel the user to submit written evidence of what they do. Continuous integrity validation helps organizations to have active compliance controls that will be in operation throughout the whole lifecycle of artifacts since their creation.

Continuous integration and continuous delivery pipelines have a major structure centering on two aspects that include artifact integrity and version traceability. The process converts build outputs of temporary technical outputs to permanent validated assets that are auditable. Companies can reach full traceability of the deployed components using their immutable systems, as well as cryptographic validation and structured versioning and chain-of-custody records. This is a feature that the digital ecosystem needs since it is subject to strict regulations. The system also provides the needed technological infrastructure that underlies change management processes and audit preparation activity and determines supply chain reliability. The level of compliance with regulations can also be measured by artifact integrity by which the organization will be able to address the compliance requirements in a defensible way and ensure compliance monitoring continues.

2.5 Secure Source Code Management and Access Controls

The first and most important security control in the software development process for compliance-driven DevOps environments exists through secure source code management. Source code repositories serve as the origin point for all artifacts and deployments and operational results. Weak governance at this basic level results in insufficient downstream controls which affect the build and testing and deployment processes. Unauthorized code changes and misuse of privileges and internal system manipulation and repository breaches create security weaknesses which spread unnoticed through automated systems. Secure source code management needs to function as a development collaboration tool while serving as a controlled system which records all activities according to established policies and maintains audit capabilities. The combination of access controls and identity governance and traceability mechanisms and configuration safeguards establishes source repositories as reliable compliance foundations which support CI/CD environments(Chase, 2025).

2.5.1 Repository Governance and Structural Controls

Secure source code management begins with structured repository governance. Repository organization needs to establish ownership boundaries which define who will maintain the system and enforce operational rules. All repositories need to follow correct categorization methods which include public and private and internal repositories to avoid accidental disclosure of confidential code. Repository management depends on branch protection policies which serve as their foundational element. Direct commits need to be banned for all essential branches which include main and release and production branches. All modifications need to be implemented through governed pull requests or merge requests which require assessment and approval. The core codebases will only allow integration after developers conduct both assessment and authorization processes. Development teams need to follow repository settings which create uniform rules for their work processes. Organizations that permit their teams to configure their work environments without restrictions create a situation where they will face challenges because different teams will apply their rules in different ways. Centralized governance frameworks maintain consistent security measures while they minimize the chances of system errors which arise from improper setup. Repository security procedures use structured governance to change version control systems into environments which guarantee compliance instead of allowing informal teamwork.

2.5.2 Identity Verification and Strong Authentication

Secure source code management depends on verified identities as the basic security pillar. The system has to give each contributor a unique identifier that can only be accessed by users with verified credentials. Those organizations that depend on weak authentication methods, such as shared accounts and systems that allow password, only access, will have difficulties in tracking user activities while their security systems will also lack monitoring capabilities. Multi, factor authentication (MFA) should secure every user of the repository, as well as more specifically users with greater access privileges should be taken into consideration during this implementation. It has the advantage that user lifecycle management is unified by integrating with an enterprise identity provider and this enables automatic system synchronization to perform user onboarding and offboarding operations. Commit signatures are a means of strengthening the identity verification process. Authors will have a way to prove their rights via cryptographic commit signatures while others will be prevented from impersonating them. Before a pull request is merged, the system checks for the signature of the contributor to ensure that this person is a certified user who has undergone the required authentication process. With a strong security baseline, authentication solutions revert source control activities to traceable user actions documented and thus security provisions and compliance requirements are being met by the organization.

2.5.3 Role-Based Access Control and Least Privilege

The system requires that role-based access control (RBAC) must control access to repositories following the least privilege access rule. Developers need access only to the repositories which their job duties require. Only a small group of users should receive administrative privileges which require monitoring. The system needs to establish separate roles which will provide different read, write, merge, and administrative rights. Users who receive excessively broad access rights will create a higher risk for both unintentional and intentional abuse of their access rights. The organization needs to conduct regular access evaluations which will verify that current access rights correspond with existing work duties. The organization needs to implement duties separation at every repository location. The change approval authority should ensure that its authority to disapprove any changes that need to be evaluated is not diminished. The repository managers are not supposed to be given the authority to alter basic application code unless they are given permission by their counterparts. The automated access assessments and the human resource system integration provide the system with automated access evaluations that keep the permission change in line with role change or termination of employees and helps in preventing insider threats.

2.5.4 Secure Pull Request and Code Review Processes

Code review mechanisms are also used as quality assurance and compliance controls. Protected pull request processes prevent the merging of changes in secure branches without being reviewed by independent personnel. The automated verification of the requirements of the reviewers is a protective measure against self-approval and evading the review.

Validation of: should be done in review processes: Adherence to secure coding standards

- Detection of hardcoded secrets or credentials
- Confirmation of test coverage
- Verification of architectural consistency

Automated tools integrated into pull request workflows can augment human review by scanning for vulnerabilities, license violations, and policy breaches before approval. The review activities should be recorded and stored, which means they include the identity of reviewers, their timestamps, reviewer comments, and their approval. These records are part of the compliance evidence trail, and they reveal compliance with the structured change management practices.

2.5.5 Protection Against Malicious or Accidental Code Injection

Malicious attackers treat source repositories as their main targets for conducting injection attacks. Attackers will try to insert backdoors while they disable logging functions and create security weaknesses, which they will present as normal software updates. The organization implements mandatory static application security testing (SAST), which testing teams must perform during both commit and pull request stages. The system uses automated scanning to identify insecure coding patterns and dangerous functions before the software undergoes integration. Repositories should undergo continuous scanning by secrets detection tools that search for exposed credentials. The system will automatically generate alerts together with remediation workflows when it detects secrets. Anomaly detection systems help identify unusual patterns of contribution through their ability to detect new account owners who make excessive commits during non-standard working times. Organizations use behavioral monitoring to create an extra security barrier that protects against insider threats and compromised account attacks.

2.5.6 Repository Integrity and Tamper Protection

Repository integrity requires protection of all components, which include source code, configuration settings, access logs, and historical revisions. Version control systems maintain change histories as their default function, yet these change records need protection to keep them secure. The system should record all administrative actions, which include force pushes, branch deletions, and history rewrites. Organizations working in regulated industries need to disable history rewriting on their critical branches because unauthorized changes need to remain visible. Organizations protect their data from loss and ransomware attacks through regular repository data backups. The organization needs to perform scheduled backup integrity checks because this process ensures it can assess the backups' capacity to support restoration activities. Organizations achieve repository integrity protection through their protection of source code, which serves as their software development reference material.

2.5.7 Integration with Compliance and Audit Frameworks

The secure source code management system provides direct support for meeting compliance needs, which require organizations to manage their system access controls and change management procedures, and protect their system operations. Regulatory expectations typically mandate:

- Controlled access to system components
- Documented change approval processes
- Traceable authorship of modifications
- Evidence of security review practices

The implementation of governance controls inside repository workflows enables organizations to produce ongoing evidence of their compliance status. Organizations can organize their audit process through approved repository logs and documentation that contains their approval records. The process of mapping repository controls to regulatory requirements creates a stronger connection between governance practices and organizational controls. Organizations can establish their compliance objectives through specific compliance requirements that connect to each implemented branch protection rule, access restriction, and review requirement.

2.5.8 Continuous Monitoring and Access Review

The management of source code through smart systems requires ongoing changes because it cannot establish fixed procedures. The team operations and project requirements create new control measures that need ongoing monitoring for their effective use. The organization conducts access reviews at set intervals to verify current authorization levels with required access rights. The reporting process uses automated systems to detect inactive user accounts and users with excessive permissions. Security teams need to evaluate repository configurations on a regular basis to check if branch protection measures and review processes remain secure. Organizations need to establish incident response plans that include their repository-level containment methods. The organizations must establish procedures to suspend accounts and revoke tokens while they work to investigate any suspicious activities. The continuous validation process enables repository governance to adapt according to evolving security threats and organizational changes.

The foundational elements of compliance-based DevOps environments start with access controls, together with secure source code management solutions. Organizations can ensure that source control systems become secure and auditable systems of record by implementing structured repository governance, strong identity verification, least-privilege access, and controlled review processes. The system enables complete tracking of all commits while establishing valid reasons for all merges, together with the ability to verify all configuration changes. The approach protects software delivery through secure digital environments, which defend against both internal and external security threats. The strict management of source code access, together with its secured integrity, establishes trustworthy controls for building, testing, and deploying processes that create a dependable delivery system that meets compliance requirements.

Multiple Choice Questions (MCQs)

1. **What is the primary objective of automated build and test governance in CI/CD pipelines?**
   A. Increase deployment frequency
   B. Reduce manual testing effort
   C. Ensure consistency, quality, and policy enforcement
   D. Minimize infrastructure costs

2. **Which tool is commonly used for automated CI/CD pipeline orchestration?**
   A. MySQL
   B. Docker Hub
   C. Jenkins
   D. Photoshop

3. **A compliance-first pipeline architecture primarily focuses on:**
   A. Speed of deployment
   B. Regulatory and policy enforcement from the start
   C. Reducing team size
   D. Eliminating documentation

4. **Which compliance standard is commonly integrated into secure DevOps pipelines for information security management?**
   A. ISO 27001
   B. HTML5
   C. CSS3
   D. REST API

5. **Which of the following is a common security threat in CI/CD pipelines?**

    A. Code refactoring

    B. Hardcoded credentials in source code

    C. Unit testing

    D. Continuous monitoring

6. **What is an effective mitigation strategy against supply chain attacks in pipelines?**

    A. Disabling logging

    B. Skipping dependency updates

    C. Implementing dependency scanning and signing

    D. Allowing unrestricted repository access

7. **Artifact integrity ensures that:**

    A. Code is written in a specific language

    B. Artifacts remain unchanged and verifiable after creation

    C. Testing is optional

    D. Deployment is manual

8. **Which technique improves artifact traceability in CI/CD pipelines?**

    A. Manual version naming

    B. Removing metadata

    C. Using version control tagging and immutable repositories

    D. Deleting old builds immediately

9. **What is the best practice for securing source code repositories?**
   A. Shared administrator accounts
   B. Public write access
   C. Role-Based Access Control (RBAC)
   D. Disabling authentication
10. **Multi-Factor Authentication (MFA) in source code management systems helps to:**
   A. Speed up builds
   B. Provide an additional security verification layer
   C. Reduce storage costs
   D. Replace encryption

Answers

1	2	3	4	5	6	7	8	9	10
C	C	B	A	B	C	B	C	C	B

Chapter 3

Automating Compliance and Policy Enforcement

3.1 POLICY-AS-CODE AND AUTOMATED CONTROL ENFORCEMENT

The current speed of software delivery in modern DevOps systems exceeds the development rate of traditional compliance and governance systems. The combination of static policy documents and periodic control reviews with manual approval workflows fails to control the operations of dynamic infrastructure, automated deployments, and continuously evolving application architectures. The implementation of Policy-as-Code (PaC) allows organizations to transform their governance requirements into machine-executable rules, which they can embed directly into their CI/CD pipelines. The delivery process uses PaC to automate control enforcement, which serves as a built-in function that operates through the delivery process. The compliance-driven DevOps model uses Policy-as-Code to create an architectural system that assesses all code commits, infrastructure definitions, and deployment decisions against established regulatory, security, and operational requirements before they enter production. (Queen, 2025).

3.1.1 Foundational Principles of Policy-as-Code

Policy-as-Code suggests an approach in which governments consider all their rules as software parts. Organizations specify their controls in formal machine-readable syntaxes and no longer rely on narrative documents to be interpreted. The policies create system requirements, comprising restrictions and permissions, configuration baselines, and anticipated system behaviour. Through this approach, since the existing software engineering techniques can be applied in governance, they bring benefits. The peer review and testing can be used to manage versions of policies used by organizations, and it is compatible with automated deployment. The process generates clarity of explanation that makes the work complete and gives the same results in various environments. The fact that written rules are replaced with executable logic erases any difference between documented rules and real implementation systems. The principle stipulates that the DevOps controls should be made mandatory systems that automatically apply compliance standards with regard to this code.

3.1.2 From Manual Oversight to Deterministic Enforcement

The traditional compliance systems depend on their capacity to perform audits through retrospective assessments and their need for human monitoring. The organization conducts control assessments at scheduled intervals, which take place after its infrastructure systems and production applications have been launched. The organization uses a reactive method, which creates two problems because it exposes operational risks and forces the business to spend more money on fixing security issues. The Policy-as-Code automated system has an automated enforcement system that does not involve any human participation. To ensure that all rules are taken care of, the system performs automatic policy checks on all pipeline executions. The system will stop or suspend deployments based on the level of their severity whenever their settings do not meet set standards.

Deterministic enforcement has several advantages for the organizations. Misconfigurations can be detected immediately. Prevention of non-compliant deployments

- Reduction of human error
- Continuous validation rather than periodic review

Compliance thus becomes an integral part of the deployment workflow, not an external checkpoint applied after the fact.

3.1.3 Control Abstraction and Regulatory Mapping

The regulatory frameworks and industry standards specify control goals that are essential and require organizations to have secure system setups, access control systems, and data protection measures. The objectives require specific technical rules that measure performance to establish automatic enforcement procedures. Organizations can use the Policy-as-Code control abstraction system to transform their policies into executable code. Organizations create enforceable regulatory conditions by decomposing requirements into specific rules, which include encryption mandates, network segmentation restrictions, identity management rules, logging requirements, and configuration baselines.

The mapping process consists of the following elements.

- Identifying regulatory clauses
- Defining measurable technical criteria
- Encoding criteria into policy definitions
- Linking policies to specific enforcement points

The result establishes a direct link that connects regulatory requirements to the enforcement procedures used in pipeline operations. Organizations can demonstrate their compliance during audits by providing proof of their existing controls together with their system, which automatically enforces security measures throughout all stages of their deployment process.

3.1.4 Core Architecture of a Policy-as-Code Framework

The implementation of a strong Policy-as-Code system needs an architectural framework that must be established as its essential base. The main elements of the system usually contain:

- **Policy Repository:** The official governance rule repository stores its documents in the centralized storage system, which uses version control as its main management system. The repository enables auditors to track changes that are managed through established protocols.

- **Policy Engine:** When configurations are compared with evaluation components, they interpret policy definitions based on the comparison.
- **Integration Points within CI/CD Pipelines:** Delivery workflows contain multiple stages, which include enforcement checkpoints as their embedded security checkpoints.
- **Logging and Evidence Capture Systems:** The system records all policy evaluations together with their corresponding decisions and violations to establish a permanent compliance audit trail. The software delivery lifecycle needs these elements to operate as a governance control plane because they work together as one system.

3.1.5 Layered Enforcement Across the CI/CD Lifecycle

Proper Policy-as-Code implementation can place safeguards at various stages in code delivery and synchronization.

- **Pre-Commit and Development Stage:** The current system enables developers to receive direct feedback from policies while they write code, which helps them find potential violations before they become actual problems.
- **Build and Integration Stage:** Before artifacts undergo packaging, the verification of dependencies, configuration parameters, and artifacts is performed.
- **Pre-Deployment Stage:** Infrastructure definitions are evaluated prior to provisioning resources.
- **Runtime Admission and Post-Deployment Monitoring:** The policies impose run-time environment limits as they track system configuration modifications. The approach of enforcement in multi-layers reduces the level of security risks as the violation of rules is detected at the earliest time possible,

leading to continuous security checking in the whole system development process.

3.1.6 Automated Testing and Validation of Policies

Application code should be tested as policy definitions are to ensure they are exactly performed and that they will perform reliably. The flawed reasoning of the policy system permits the occurrence of acts that are not permitted, as well as hinders the functionality of the system.

The testing policies process entails the following approaches:

- Unit testing individual rules
- Regression testing to prevent unintended logic changes
- Simulation testing using representative configurations
- Continuous integration testing within pipeline environments

Automated testing strengthens policy reliability and ensures that enforcement mechanisms remain aligned with regulatory requirements as systems evolve.

3.1.7 Policy Lifecycle Management and Governance

Policy-as-Code implementation should have a governance practice that organizes its entire lifecycle to prevent the development of impactful and fragmented outputs. A company must come up with a lifecycle structure that has the following:

- Formal drafting and documentation of policies
- Peer review and approval workflows
- Version tracking and change logs
- Rollback mechanisms for rapid correction
- Archival processes for historical traceability

Lifecycle governance ensures that policies remain synchronized with regulatory updates and organizational risk strategies. The investigation result and evidence must be recorded as permissible evidence, utilizable evidence or direct evidence.

3.1.8 Risk-Based Enforcement and Severity Classification

Not every policy violation can be equally risky. The PaC framework deploys risk-based classification models with high levels of sophistication in order to balance the governance needs of its framework and the efficiency with which it must perform. The following types of violations exist:

- Critical (deployment blocked automatically)
- High-risk (manual approval required)
- Moderate (warning with remediation guidance)
- Informational (logged for visibility)

This is a systematic process of avoidable disruption to the operations besides keeping the high-impact controls strict.

3.1.9 Exception Handling and Governance Overrides

Changes in standard controls are only to be done when business necessities request it to be so. Policy-as-Code frameworks should be set up to have an organized way of managing exceptions. Exception governance process must contain the following elements:

- Formal approval mechanisms
- Time-bound exemptions
- Documented justification
- Automated expiration of overrides
- Continuous monitoring of exception usage

By codifying exceptions, organizations preserve flexibility while ensuring accountability and traceability.

3.1.10 Policy-as-Code/Compliance-as-Code.

The Policy roles, as Code and Compliance, interact as they are both concerned with one mission. The essence of Policy, as Code is to create security standards that will be introduced across the operational and architectural fields. The Compliance, as Code framework improves its operation by converting regulatory provisions into control standards and official reports that can be measured.

In DevOps based on compliance:

- Policy-as-Code operationalizes enforcement.
- Compliance-as-Code provides regulatory alignment and audit reporting.

Together, they form a cohesive governance automation strategy.

3.1.11 Continuous Compliance Monitoring and Audit Readiness

The major advantage of Policy-as-Code systems is that they can be automatically created to produce evidence of their operations. The system generates structured metadata at every assessment occasion that includes dates and rule numbers and remediation information and result of evaluation.

Such records constitute a running record of compliance that justifies: Real-time visibility into control adherence

- Historical traceability of enforcement decisions
- Audit preparation without manual evidence collection
- Capability for good governance delivery

Continuous monitoring provides real-time compliance assessment which enables ongoing monitoring of compliance status instead of waiting for audit periods to conduct assessments.

3.1.12 Organizational and Cultural Transformation

Policy-as-Code implementation ties together compliance needs with engineering processes that leads to organizations to shift their inner working mechanisms. Governance requirements may be seen by developers, policy engineers may be security personnel, and compliance officers may get automatic reporting and evidence documentation.

This transformation develops: Policy-as-Code implementation ties together compliance needs with engineering processes that leads to organizations to shift their inner working mechanisms. Governance requirements may be seen by developers, policy engineers may be security personnel, and compliance officers may get automatic reporting and evidence documentation.

This transformation develops:

- Shared responsibility for compliance
- Reduced friction between teams
- Increased operational transparency
- Improved collaboration between governance and engineering functions

Compliance becomes embedded in daily development practices rather than treated as an external constraint.

Policy-as-Code has introduced a novel set of governance practices in DevOps settings. In the process of transforming regulatory requirements into operational rules, organizations attain continuous compliance using automated compliance enforcement that its CI/CD pipelines implement. To ensure the system is ready to face audits, automated evidence creation is used to prepare, and deterministic validation replaces periodic assessment and risk-based enforcement provides a tradeoff between governance demands and operational flexibility. Policy-as-Code is the key system that ensures that compliance requirements are automatically enforced during all stages of delivered software in compliance-dependent delivery pipelines.

3.2 INFRASTRUCTURE AS CODE FOR COMPLIANCE CONSISTENCY

Infrastructure as Code (IaC) is a framework that allows organizations to run their infrastructure resources via an automated engineering process, combining version control with full auditing capabilities. A DevOps setup demanding compliance with certain regulations relies on IaC as its main automation tool to create infrastructure systems, which can be verified time and again according to established policies. Compliance, wise, organizations have machines that can read the configuration files that lay out their infrastructure and then use these to form their delivery pipelines, which ensure their systems are compliant while also generating audit documentation continuously. Here, the focus is on how IaC assists organizations in achieving compliance because it does so by joining governance and traceability with control validation in their infrastructure provisioning processes (Holdsworth & Badman, 2025).

3.2.1 Defining Infrastructure as Code in a Compliance Context

Infrastructure as Code is the practice of provisioning and managing infrastructure, including networks, compute resources, storage and platform services, and security configurations, using declarative or imperative configuration files, which are managed in version control systems. The traditional definitions are focused on automation and speed whereas a compliance-focused interpretation is based on determinism, repeatability and traceability.

In controlled setting, infrastructure should be based on predefined configuration baselines. Common standards to which these baselines can conform include ISO 27001 configuration controls, NIST system integrity requirements or CIS benchmark recommendations. IaC enables these base lines to be template codified. Each deployment made with such templates is a managed copy of a verified state and removes unofficial deviations and informal settings.

Instead of viewing infrastructure as a dynamic space that constantly changes, IaC requires infrastructure to be managed and treated as a controlled artifact: reviewed, approved, versioned and reproducible.

- The Core Characteristics of Infrastructure as Code enable organizations to maintain conformity with regulatory requirements.

The basic nature of Infrastructure as Code systems brings automatic regulatory compliance to their operations.

The Continuous Integration and Continuous Deployment (CI/CD) system uses pipelines to automatically test and validate and deploy infrastructure changes. This is so as to make sure that all changes go through standard approval and validation procedures that help in providing audit needs on change management and separation of duties.

Modularity and Reusability: Reusable infrastructure modules eliminate duplication and limit configuration variation. Approved compliance modules could be reused in other teams where it is always ensured a secure configuration is being applied on an enterprise-wide basis.

Idempotency: Idempotent infrastructure definition ensures that a configuration can be used multiple times with identical results. It is a critical property as it is needed to validate compliance as it guarantees predictable system states, which are deterministic.

Immutable Infrastructure: Compliant infrastructure practices assume that outdated components are replaced with new approved components by replacing live systems with new ones. This method eases the rollback, forensic investigation and audit trail as well as reduces configuration drift.

3.2.2 IaC as a Mechanism for Risk Reduction

Human error is still among the greatest factors that contribute to security incidents. The process of manual configuration leads to operational problems through the introduction of outdated changes and system errors which include open ports and improperly configured access controls. The use of IaC technology results in risk reduction because it replaces manual tasks with processes that operate automatically after receiving operational authorization.

Infrastructure templates can establish compliance controls which include encryption requirements and network segregation rules and logging standards and identity management specifications. The system automatically enforces compliance controls when users execute these templates. The system eliminates the need for manual checklists which decreases the probability of security vulnerabilities through control weaknesses.

The compliance validation process for organizations now starts during infrastructure provisioning because this method enables organizations to detect potential violations before they reach audit evaluation stage.

3.2.3 Version Control as an Audit Evidence System

The main advantage of Infrastructure as Code for maintaining compliance requirements comes from its ability to connect with version control systems. The infrastructure definitions which repositories store deliver the following benefits to organizations:

- Complete historical records of changes
- Author attribution for each modification
- Timestamped approvals
- Peer review documentation
- Traceable rollback capability

These attributes directly support regulatory requirements for change management documentation. The organization can show when a configuration was introduced to the system because they have documentation which shows who authorized it and which controls their system deployed. The complete history of infrastructure information becomes permanent record because it functions as ongoing proof which security experts use to verify system integrity.

However, since IaC lacks Governance and Compliance Controls, they need to be embedded.

The code architecture is able to transform the indicators of governance hierarchies into the enforceable operations. Examples are as follows:

- Mandatory encryption for storage resources
- Logging enabled for all network endpoints
- Multi-factor authentication enforced for administrative access
- Restricted security group rules

- Standardized tagging for asset classification

When governance rules are embedded in IaC modules, compliance enforcement becomes automatic. The pipeline validation process enables non-compliant infrastructure definitions to be rejected before they get into the production environments.

The system achieves compliance through two mechanisms which work together to establish executable infrastructure definitions that match governance policies.

3.2.4 Preventing and Detecting Configuration Drift

Configuration drift happens when environments lose their original state because of manual modifications and uncoordinated updates. Drift undermines compliance consistency because systems can become mismatched with their established baseline standards.

The two main ways that IaC controls drift are through the following methods:

1. The reconciliation mechanisms of the system perform ongoing comparisons between actual operational infrastructure and its specified configuration state.
2. The system uses unchangeable replacement methods which require no in-between system updates.

The system uses drift detection tools which work together with its pipelines to provide automated alerts that detect all discrepancies between expected and actual results. The alerts function as compliance monitoring tools which allow organizations to fix issues quickly while their systems remain ready for audits.

3.2.5 Testing and Validating Infrastructure for Compliance

If the software below is tested automatically, why not use infrastructure code to validate tests?

- Static configuration analysis
- Security misconfiguration scanning

- Policy compliance validation
- Integration testing in isolated environments

The testing process requires verification that all infrastructure definitions meet applicable regulatory standards which must be confirmed before deployment. The organization uses preventive testing methods because they decrease remediation expenses while enhancing their governance capabilities.

The infrastructure testing frameworks enable organizations to test their deployment systems through sandbox environments which allow them to verify their encryption policies, access controls and network boundaries before releasing the system to production.

3.2.6 Managing Change Through Small, Controlled Updates

Large, tightly coupled infrastructure changes increase risk and complicate compliance oversight. IaC encourages small, incremental, and independently testable changes.

Smaller change sets provide:

- Clearer audit trails
- Easier rollback capabilities
- Reduced blast radius in case of failure
- Simplified compliance validation

The organization establishes a system to decrease regulatory compliance requirements through its implementation of infrastructure upgrades as separate trackable elements.

3.2.7 Integrating IaC with Policy-as-Code

The implementation of infrastructure definitions requires organizations to validate their systems through testing. The system requirements need to be verified through testing against established organizational standards. The system requires testing infrastructure changes through Policy-as-Code frameworks which will evaluate these changes to the established rules before their implementation.

This layered approach establishes a dual-control model:

- IaC defines the desired infrastructure state.
- Policy-as-Code validates that the state complies with governance standards.

Together, they create a self-enforcing compliance ecosystem embedded within the CI/CD pipeline.

3.2.8 IaC as a Foundation for Immutable and Ephemeral Environments

Contemporary cloud-native systems and their container workloads require temporary computing resources, which are created through dynamic resource creation. The use of manual control becomes impossible within these operational environments.

The Infrastructure as Code system creates temporary environments that automatically receive compliant configuration settings. The system uses approved templates to create temporary environments, which guarantees that all development, testing, and production systems will maintain uniformity.

The ability to reproduce results remains crucial for audits and incident investigations and disaster recovery operations. The use of versioned templates enables organizations to recreate their environments as they existed at a particular moment in time.

3.2.9 Applying Software Engineering Discipline to Infrastructure Code

The infrastructure code should also be treated with the same rigor as an application code. Which encompasses:

- Peer review processes
- Code quality checks
- Documentation standards
- Testing coverage
- Technical debt management

Poorly maintained infrastructure code introduces compliance risk just as vulnerable application code does. The combination of a disciplined engineering culture with its established operational procedures leads to sustainable organizational success which also helps the organization comply with industry regulations.

Organizations use Infrastructure as Code as an automation solution which helps them achieve governance by automatically complying with their delivery pipeline processes. The implementation of infrastructure baselines through codification together with validation processes in CI/CD workflows and configuration drift prevention measures and continuous audit evidence generation establishes consistency for IaC across all changing environments.

The combination of Infrastructure as Code with Policy-as-Code and structured change management processes enables organizations to implement audit-compliant DevOps practices which convert infrastructure into a transparent system that organizations can use to track their regulatory compliance.

3.3 Managing Secrets, Credentials, and Sensitive Data

The machines in the contemporary DevOps environment can be seen to communicate with each other more than the human being communicates with the systems. CI/CD pipelines connect cloud platforms, containers fetch images on registries, microservices invoke external APIs, and automation scripts provide authentication against databases and infrastructure elements. All of these interactions need credentials, API keys, tokens, certificates, encryption keys, and service account passwords. When not managed, these digital secrets turn out to be one of the most exploited attack vectors when it comes to the enterprise setting. Secrets management is not just a security improvement in a compliance-based DevOps model but a governance requirement. This segment examines how companies can develop and result flawless administration of secrets, automate, and execute secure administration over secrets to provide audit preparedness, minimize intrusion, and provide policy-worthy accessaining delivery pipelines(Holdsworth, 2025).

3.3.1 Understanding Secrets in the DevOps and Cloud-Native Context

Secrets are digital credentials that are sensitive and allow authentication, authorization, and secure communication between systems. They are passwords, SSH keys, API tokens, encryption keys, TLS certificates, OAuth tokens, database credentials and identities of service accounts. In contrast to classic user credentials, applications, automation tools, containers and background services consume many secrets, and they are more difficult to monitor and control. Secret keys in cloud native and CI/CD-driven environments are decided in automated processes. When not managed correctly, they can leak in source repositories, environment variables, build logs, container images or configuration files. Since such credentials tend to provide privileged access, their compromise may result in a lateral movement, data exfiltration or an infrastructure takeover. Compliance-wise, secrets are valuable control points. Industrial standards like ISO 27001, NIST models, SOC 2, PCI-DSS, and GDPR demand close management of the keys to sensitive systems and data. The management of secrets becomes then a necessary tool to implement the identity governance and to illustrate the regulatory compliance.

3.3.2 The Secret Lifecycle: Governance from Creation to Revocation

The management of secrets needs to have a structured lifecycle management. The secret does not exist, but it passes through certain phases:

1. **Creation or Generation** - The generation of secrets must be done with high standards of cryptography and not manually created or recycled.
2. **Storage** - Secrets should be saved in centralized vault systems in encrypted format as opposed to code repositories or configuration files.
3. **Access and Usage-** The access must be role and policy-based access control within the Principle of Least Privilege (PoLP).

4. **Rotation** -There should be periodic rotation of secrets so as to reduce the exposure period in case of a compromise.
5. **Monitoring and Auditing-** All the access attempts should be registered and trackable.
6. **Revocation and Expiration -** Secrets have to be revoked when they are not needed or when suspicious activity is observed.

Organizations minimize human error by codifying and automating this lifecycle to provide consistency in the enforcement of compliance across environments.

3.3.3 Risks of Poor Secrets Management in DevOps Pipelines

Inadequate handling of secrets poses a great compliance and security risk:

- **Hardcoded Credentials:** Embedding secrets in source code or scripts results in long-term vulnerability. When the repositories are exposed, the attackers have instant access to the system. Hardcoded credentials also make rotation challenging and can be demanding in terms of code changes across multiple locations.
- **Secrets Sprawl:** The ad hoc storage used by distributed teams of ad hoc storage consortium results in fragmented and unmanaged inventories of secrets which creates security problems. The system becomes entirely impossible to control because its components become hidden from view.
- **Stale or Unrotated Credentials:** The combination of stale credentials together with unrotated credentials creates security vulnerabilities because long-lived credentials remain active indefinitely. Hackers can use secrets compromised in long durations without being noticed.
- **CI/CD Exposure:** Build logs together with container layers and artifact repositories present a danger because they can contain confidential data. The danger increases because workers in fast-paced environments must handle confidential information through secret processing methods.

- **Third-Party Access Risks:** The vendors and partners receive shared credentials which lead to third-party access risks because they possess limited control over third-party secret management practices. The internal risk may come in as a result of weak security practices outside the organization.

Under compliance-based settings, organizations face direct financial consequences from risks which result in both audit findings and regulatory penalties and damage to their reputation.

3.3.4 Centralized Vault Architecture for Compliance Consistency

The secret vault must function as a central system to establish secure DevOps governance. The vault system also allows companies to securely retain credentials in their encrypted storage system as well as allowing controlled access and automating workflow.

The basic components of a compliant system design of a vault are the following features:

The system should have encryption at rest by use of high standards of cryptography. Encryption in transit via secure transport protocols

- Strict authentication and authorization controls
- API-driven secret retrieval
- Immutable audit logs
- High availability and resilience

Centralization makes sure that there are no longer secrets in the application code as well as secrets distributed manually. Pipelines and applications require credentials to be gained in the process of execution. The model can guarantee the level of compliance through access restrictions that are made uniform and generate trace records of secret access.

Role-Based Access Control and the Principle of Least Privilege

For example:

The secrets management must implement elaborate access controls that enable specific access rights to be given to the users. Role-Based Access Control (RBAC) allocates permission based on the job roles, whereas rules of the policy limit access based on time, circumstance, or environment.

- The developers have development credentials that enable them to read but not to make changes in the system.
- Operations teams have the authority to control their rotation policies.
- Security teams have the authorization to examine access logs for their auditing purposes.
- The CI/CD pipelines actually need to have temporary tokens that they can utilize in making their build.

Least privilege access controls will reduce the possible attack points and will not violate the identity governance requirements. The system also enables organizations to maintain duty separation which serves as an essential regulatory requirement across multiple industries.

3.3.5 Dynamic Secrets and Just-in-Time Access

The use of traditional static credentials creates persistent security hazards throughout their entire existence. The development of dynamic secrets solves this problem because they create temporary credentials which users need for particular tasks. The system generates credentials which will become invalid after the specified time duration.

For instance:

- A pipeline job receives a database credential which remains valid for one hour.
- A container obtains a temporary API token which lasts until the container completes its startup process.

- An automation service account receives temporary access rights which permit access to specific functions for a defined period.

Dynamic secret models create shorter periods during which attackers can exploit systems. Intercepted credentials lose their value after they reach their expiration date. The use of short-lived credentials shows active risk management while organizations maintain their advanced security control capabilities.

3.3.6 Automated Rotation and Revocation Mechanisms

The system automatically rotates secured information at regular intervals which requires no human input for its operation. The security framework determines different times for rotating sensitive information based on its protection level and legal obligations and its specific security threat patterns.

Automated rotation provides several compliance advantages:

- Reduced exposure time for compromised credentials
- Elimination of human-dependent processes
- Consistent enforcement across environments
- Simplified audit reporting

Revocation capabilities allow immediate invalidation of secrets during incidents or employee exits. Incident Response frameworks seek to be agile with minimal complexities, ensuring that audits are systematically completed.

3.3.7 Secure Secret Injection into CI/CD Pipelines

Secrets must not be embedded into pipelines through permanent storage methods or through direct manual entry. The system uses secure injection methods to access secrets which it retrieves from vault systems during runtime operations.

Secure injection principles include:

- API-based retrieval during job execution

- In-memory usage without file persistence
- Automatic cleanup after pipeline completion
- Masking of secret values in logs
- Avoid storing secrets in container layers

By automating injection, organizations reduce exposure risk and align pipeline operations with compliance policies. By proper management of secrets, it is good to ensure that they are available to use when needed and that they are destroyed once the operational time is over.

3.3.8 Audit Logging and Compliance Evidence

Complete audit logging must have its objective of facilitating regulatory compliance achieved. The system should generate a safe record of all the efforts to access a secret and these are successful attempts and failed attempts.

The logs should include the following information:

- Identity of requester
- Secret accessed
- Timestamp
- Source IP or system
- Action performed (read, update, revoke)

Centralized logging enables:

- Real-time anomaly detection
- Incident investigation
- Forensic reconstruction
- Automated compliance reporting

Immutable audit trails provide defensible evidence during external audits and demonstrate continuous monitoring of privileged access.

3.3.9 Segregation of Environments and Data Sensitivity

You must have various secret repositories of your development and staging as well as production. Reuse of the same credentials in various environment poses security threats besides violating access control policies.

It should also have several stages of secrecy classification of the material. The credentials that are high-risk like encryption keys to regulated data must have tighter rotation settings, watch dogs and approval processes.

The hierarchical system of segregation defends against inadvertent disclosure even as it enhances the governance practices at the entire organization.

3.3.10 Combining Secrets management with Widening Governance Structures

The management of secrets should be combined with:

Identity and Access Management (IAM) systems

- Privileged Access Management (PAM) controls
- Security Information and Event Management (SIEM) platforms
- Incident response workflows
- Policy-as-Code validation engines

The integration will ensure the enterprise risk management strategies will have an adequate secret governance with its implementation. The system involves automatic notifications in order to identify abnormal secret usage that triggers incident response mechanisms that improve compliance status of the.

3.3.11 Establishing a Compliance-Driven Secret Governance Model

The following provisions should be included in a mature secrets management program:

- Clear ownership of secret lifecycle processes
- Documented policies for creation, storage, rotation, and deletion
- Regular access reviews
- Automated compliance checks
- Periodic penetration testing focused on secret exposure
- Continuous improvement based on audit findings

The maturity of governance keeps growing with time, but automation still plays in the center, for scalability and consistent support.

The process of managing secret information and sensitive credentials and private data constitutes one of the fundamental compliance requirements that DevOps must follow. The use of automated pipelines and machine-to-machine connections becomes more common in enterprises which creates a security risk because hackers can exploit unmanaged credentials to breach their advanced security systems. The implementation of centralized vault systems together with least privilege access controls and rotation and revocation abilities and CI/CD injection mechanisms and audit trails will enable organizations to transform secret management into a measurable governance practice. The system enables organizations to build delivery pipelines that maintain compliance with regulatory requirements while providing an auditing system that operates at all times.

3.4 CONTINUOUS COMPLIANCE MONITORING AND VALIDATION

The organizations that exist today handle compliance requirements as an intermittent necessity, which they fulfill through extensive work that occurs during their audit and regulatory review periods. The staff at these organizations must spend their time away from essential work duties during the periods of audit operations to collect needed records and fix existing issues. The organization employs a maintenance method that results in work interruptions and emergency solutions that do not resolve the ongoing problems that exist between auditing periods. The current time period requires organizations to adopt permanent compliance practices because of the ongoing technological improvements, increasing regulatory requirements and rising cybersecurity threats. Organizations need to move from conducting sporadic checks to implementing ongoing supervision. The system of continuous compliance monitoring and validation establishes a new compliance method that demonstrates operational readiness through continuous assessment instead of providing specific time-based checks. The section examines the basic principles that drive continuous compliance and its advantages and the framework for its execution, and the technological systems that support it. The research investigates how validation systems help monitoring systems to achieve two goals, which include showing system operations and proving the effectiveness of control measures (R, 2025).

3.4.1 From Periodic Audits to Continuous Compliance

Old models of compliance are based on post facto analysis. The evaluations of controls occur once they are in effect, which is usually months after an organization discovers its vulnerability. Periodic audits can be used to detect deficiencies but often the warning is realized when the risk becomes a reality. This reactive model is substituted with an embedded and real-time model with constant compliance. Instead of affirmation at periodic intervals, organizations have incorporated regulations into working processes, information systems and software development processes.

Key distinctions include:

Table 3.1: Comparative Analysis of Traditional and Continuous Compliance Models

Traditional Compliance	Continuous Compliance
Periodic audits	Ongoing monitoring
Manual evidence collection	Automated evidence generation
Retrospective validation	Real-time detection

Reactive remediation	Proactive prevention
High audit disruption	Sustained audit readiness

Source: (R, 2025)

Continuous compliance does not eliminate audits; instead, it transforms them from high-stress events into confirmation exercises supported by continuously collected evidence.

3.4.2 Drivers of Continuous Compliance

Several structural forces necessitate this transition:

1. **Regulatory Complexity:** Organizations must follow multiple regulatory frameworks which control their operations in data protection and financial reporting and healthcare information and cybersecurity and industry-specific requirements. The quantity and particularity of demands keep growing.
2. **Technological Acceleration:** Remote work environments combined with cloud computing and distributed architectures and DevOps practices both imply dynamically changing system configurations. The compliance checking with the static requirements process does not correspond to the requirements of the systems that face constant changes in infrastructure.
3. **Evolving Cyber Threats:** Cyber threats are persistent in existence and they are evolving new strategies of attack. Organizations are exposed to serious security threats since they do not identify and resolve system vulnerabilities that occur in between their planned security audits.
4. **Reputational and Financial Risk:** The non-conformity penalties are in the form of fines enforced by the regulatory authorities and the legal penalties and interference to business operation and loss of trust of the stakeholders. The cost of reactive remediation is more than the proactive monitoring. The ever-present compliance demands by these forces give rise to a critical requirement that organizations should be able to comply.

3.4.3 Core Benefits of Continuous Compliance

Continuous compliance offers strategic, operational, and financial advantages.

- **Superior Security Posture:** Organizations use active enforcement of controls instead of using passive control documentation. The system provides organizations with instant detection capabilities, which enable them to address configuration changes and security breaches and policy violations as they occur.
- **Real-Time Visibility:** Continuous monitoring provides insights on compliance status that help take informed decisions and reduce any uncertainties.
- **Sustained Audit Readiness:** Automated evidence collection together with automated logging procedures proved to be effective in decreasing the administrative work required for audit preparation. The system generates documentation throughout the entire process instead of creating it during the final compilation phase.
- **Predictable Cost Structure:** Organizations can budget their compliance activities more effectively through two methods which include reducing emergency remediation efforts and eliminating unexpected regulatory requirements.
- **Cultural Transformation:** The implementation of compliance requirements into daily business operations creates a system which holds all employees accountable for their duties throughout different organizational departments.

3.4.4 A Seven-Step Framework for Achieving Continuous Compliance

It must be implemented in a transition and organized manner.

Step 1: Evaluation and Breakeven Analysis.

Organizations must evaluate which regulatory requirements apply to their operations and assess their existing control mechanisms. The process of formal gap analysis identifies existing deficiencies while establishing a hierarchy for necessary improvement needs.

Step 2: Policy and Process Development.

Regulatory requirements need to create rules which should define organizational roles and responsibilities together with their operational procedures. The system needs to function without interruption through its automatic monitoring features which require maximum documentation support.

Step 3: Monitoring Technologies Deployment.

The organization needs to maintain continuous compliance through its technological systems. The organization implements the following security practices:

Security Information and Event Management (SIEM) systems.

- Configuration management applications.
- Vulnerability management systems.
- Software of compliance management.

Security monitoring in cloud solutions

These are a set of systems that offer centralized administration and automated detection.

Step 4: Organizational Alignment and Training.

Compliance responsibility exists as a shared duty among all people. The training programs must focus on the practical implications, incident reporting policy, and policy compliance.

Step 5: Ongoing Monitoring and Real-Time Reporting.

The automated systems monitor system settings, access control, data streams, and security actions. The system alerts and initiates recovery processes when the users violate the set security measures.

Step 6: Continuing Auditing and Sovereign validation.

Internal audit gauges the effectiveness of control systems and monitoring. External assessment gives external accreditation that enhances the effectiveness of the governance systems.

Step 7: Feedback and Continuous Improvement.

Monitoring and audit data as well as incident analysis are incorporated in the systematic improvement cycle. The process of managing the emerging risks and impending regulatory changes develops mechanisms to the organization.

3.4.5 Compliance Validation Mechanisms

Those who support surveillance systems feel that it will offer absolute compliance. Validation is used to ensure that controls are functioning as intended and that they are producing quantifiable security assurance.

The given validation mechanisms are extremely important:

- **Control Testing:** The control testing involves the use of automated and manual testing to determine the effectiveness of controls in the actual operation conditions.
- **Evidence Collection and Retention:** Audit trails are the results of continuous logging that shows compliance during various eras and are difficult to distort.
- **Continuous Control Validation (CCV):** System settings are maintained by automated checks and scripts that have a pre-defined set of compliance standards.
- **Instant Credibility:** The third-party audits and attestation are performed to prove the internal compliance claims.
- **Exception Management:** The work processes initiate automated processes through which the staff document and tag work that has to be repaired until it is resolved completely.

Assurance is achieved through the feedback process comprising of two major parts through which they attain their objectives, which are detection and verification and remediation and confirmation.

3.4.6 Automation as the Foundation of Continuous Compliance

Automation is the principal controller of operations that allow companies to sustain continuous compliance. The sophisticated digital worlds demand 24/7 surveillance that the manual procedures cannot offer.

Automation supports:

- Real-time monitoring and alerting
- Automated policy enforcement
- Configuration drift detection
- Patch management
- Access control enforcement
- Data classification and encryption
- Automated audit trail generation
- Report generation and dashboard visualization

By reducing human error and administrative burden, automation allows compliance teams to focus on risk analysis and strategic governance rather than routine documentation.

3.4.7 Organizational and Cultural Implications

All the parts of this book are dedicated to the necessity of constant compliance, managerial support, structurally inculcated inclusion, and alignment of the culture.

Some of the significant organizational factors that must be made in order to create continuous compliance include:

Executive sponsorship

- Cross-functional coordination
- Clear accountability structures
- Integration with enterprise risk management
- Alignment with cybersecurity and IT governance

When compliance becomes embedded in daily operations rather than treated as an external imposition, organizations develop resilience rather than mere regulatory adherence.

3.4.8 Continuous Compliance as Strategic Advantage

Continuous compliance is such a concept that all regulatory requirements are turned into strategic capability. Those organizations that keep a constant preparedness will be:

- Reduced operational disruption
- Lower regulatory exposure
- Enhanced stakeholder trust
- Stronger security posture
- Greater adaptability to regulatory change

The growing digital world and the rising number of regulations require organizations to maintain ongoing compliance efforts instead of pursuing temporary compliance solutions. The activities of continuous monitoring and validation provide a reliable system that controls security requirements and risk management needs and security verification processes. Companies that adopt the continuous compliance models are able to be audit ready all through the year which forms an enduring operational competitive advantage to the business.

3.5 EXCEPTION HANDLING AND COMPLIANCE DRIFT MANAGEMENT

Compliance environments today are forced to contend with three enduring challenges that comprise the continual technological progress, the increasing regulatory demands, and the changing security threat trends. Organizations must build adaptable systems for their dynamic environments which enable them to manage access to all regulatory and internal compliance requirements. The organization needs to update its systems because of required infrastructure growth and emergency system changes, which should be treated as actual operational requirements that exist outside of established control frameworks. The organization uses mature governance practices to achieve its objectives through planned deviations which maintain transparency and accountability while managing risk through established metrics. The two governance areas of exception handling and compliance drift management operate as two interconnected domains. Exception handling deals with authorized changes that move away from standard procedures, while compliance drift management handles the process of discovering and correcting unauthorized alterations that deviate from approved standards. The two systems work together to maintain regulatory compliance while supporting business operations(Walker, 2025).

3.5.1 Conceptual Foundations of Compliance Exceptions

A compliance exception defines the authorized and recognized departure from established regulatory requirements and policy obligations and internal control standards. Exceptions occur when organizations face situations where designated controls cannot be fully implemented because of existing practical challenges and technical limitations and excessive expenses and interruptions to operational activities. Mature organizations create formal systems to handle their assessment and documentation and oversight of all their operational deviations instead of choosing to disregard those deviations. Organizations use three types of exceptions which include temporary exceptions and permanent exceptions and emergency-based exceptions. Organizations grant temporary exceptions to their systems which they are currently upgrading and their vendors which they are currently transitioning to new systems. Organizations may issue permanent exceptions when organizations show that they need full compliance but their existing controls will reduce their risk level to acceptable standards. High-pressure emergency situations such as incident response and disaster recovery require emergency exceptions because they need immediate actions to restore service. The essential aspect that distinguishes a valid exception from others lies in the organized system which controls its implementation. Organizations that handle exceptions according to established procedures show they understand risks and take responsibility for them but organizations that lack documentation of their exceptions show they have weak governance systems.

3.5.2 Exception Lifecycle and Risk Governance

The process of effective exception handling needs a dedicated system that establishes clear visibility and complete auditability for exception management. The lifecycle starts with formal identification, which usually begins after audit results or automated system checks or operational information is disclosed. The identification process requires an exception to undergo risk assessment, which determines potential damage to confidentiality and integrity and availability and regulatory compliance and financial system stability and corporate reputation.

Governance authorities must conduct their review of the exception after risk assessment completion. Approval process requires a set of documented reasons of the request, which should have given a time frame as well as acceptance of risks declarations with providing evidence of protection measures. The introduction of compensating controls sets basic operating procedures that help firms to reduce the prevailing security exposures that are caused by their inability to achieve the set security standards.

Exception records are stored in the central governance database and they are managed by the institutions over time following their official authorization. The organization should also make reassessment at frequent intervals to ensure that temporary exceptions remain as non-permanent exceptions. The system combines expiration dates and review processes alongside escalation processes to create the sense of responsibility and avoid the situation when people become careless. The two methods of closure operate through either complete remediation, which achieves full compliance or through a new authorization process that requires a reassessment of previous decisions.

The lifecycle method changes the way organizations handle exceptions because it transforms their informal procedures into formal risk management tools.

3.5.3 Governance Structures and Audit Transparency

The complete framework of governance systems needs to incorporate the process of exception handling. The system needs separate approval authority which must function independently from authorization processes and essential decisions should use defined escalation procedures to prevent unauthorized access. Executive oversight ensures that organizations will take risks which match their approved risk limits together with their operational strategic goals.

The process of documentation plays a vital role in establishing proof for legal defense. Every exception requires an explanation which includes impact assessment details and compensating control documentation together with approval documents and expiration information and monitoring requirements. The evaluation process of auditors and regulators now includes both compliance assessment and evaluation of how well organizations manage their exception handling activities. Organizations that maintain weak control over their exception management system face the risk of showing compliance yet demonstrating fundamental control weaknesses within their system.

The development of an effective exception governance system needs three key elements which include transparent processes and centralized exception tracking and automated reporting systems.

3.5.4 The Nature and Risks of Compliance Drift

Approved systems work based on a baseline configuration that outlines their intended state, however, compliance drift causes such systems to function using unapproved actual configurations. Systems undergo state drift when their current state differs from the approved state stored in the baseline. Drift detection gets harder the longer systems without continuous monitoring go as they keep the changes hidden until they become noticeable. A system can deviate significantly from its approved configuration once a series of incremental minor changes accumulates to their full impact.

There are two main reasons for drift: unauthorized changes in the system are made by the users, and organizations don't run their change management process fully. The latter includes not patching the system properly, growing the infrastructure, or simply making mistakes. Cloud-based systems and DevOps environments use rapid configuration changes, and, hence, they increase the risk of organizations losing track of system changes.

Drift puts organizations at various types of risk. Misconfiguration in the system can open up vulnerabilities that are exploited by criminals; such vulnerabilities can be prevented if the proper configuration settings are enabled. An organization can violate regulatory requirements unintentionally. The system goes through a process of decreasing reliability. The process of forensic investigation gets complicated due to the existing accumulated drift which is also the cause of reduced audit process trust. Control effectiveness fall.

3.5.5 Baseline Management and Continuous Drift Detection

Staff members who work as data analysts need to have access to all the information they require to perform their job duties. Your training includes all available data that existed before October 2023. Effective drift management requires organizations to establish clear and documented baseline standards. A baseline definition establishes the approved configuration state which includes system settings and access controls and encryption standards and network configurations and software versions. The operational state represents all currently deployed configuration settings that exist within the environment.

Detection systems of drift make use of automatic tools and monitoring systems to compare the operational conditions with their preset level standards. The system sends out alerts upon the identification of discrepancies that results in the creation of the remediation workflows. In sophisticated systems, automated correction programs will bring systems back to their authorized state without human intervention.

Baseline enforcement is designed to ensure compliance needs and create a standardized infrastructure that results in predictable operations and better cybersecurity defence in organizations. The organization identifies its configuration discipline by maintaining the organizational control by constant validation and comparison that makes it establish the control of the organization to minimize its exposure windows.

3.5.6 Snap-On Auditing and Continuous validation models

The organization adopts its drift management system by use of two validation techniques that involve snapshot-based validation and continuous validation. Snapshot auditing is used in the system to record system configuration at specified times and which can be used in future analysis and forensic examination. The technique assists in developing audit proof documentation as well as confirming disaster recovery processes. The system tracks all configuration changes as they happen in continuous validation. The system instantly identifies deviations which shortens the period organizations remain exposed to threats while enabling them to address the issue before it develops further. Organizations that combine both operational models gain advantages from their capacity to track past events and their ability to protect themselves in the present.

The two methods together create a framework which enables organizations to maintain better governance control while protecting their compliance requirements.

3.5.7 Integration with Change, Incident, and Risk Management

Exception handling and drift management need to operate together with other system components. Change management processes handle authorized system changes through their implementation into updated baseline documents and other system documentation. The detection of drift establishes a link to incident management frameworks which enable systematic process analysis and solution development. Configuration management databases (CMDBs) serve as official documentation sources that define baseline standards and show connections between different assets. The business needs to follow its enterprise risk management system to track all risk-related activities which will help with risk assessment activities.

The lack of system integration leads monitoring systems to create excessive alerts which do not solve any problems. The detection process turns into designated responsibility which leads to ongoing improvements through the integration of governance systems.

3.5.8 Automation and Scalable Control Enforcement

The process of automation serves as the essential requirement for organizations to manage exceptions and track operational changes inside their complex digital systems. The process of manual monitoring fails to provide continuous system validation which needs to operate across multiple remote systems. The automated tools in the system allow organizations to authenticate their policies, compare configuration, administer exception processing, verify their compliance with patches, and create audit trails.

Automation will result in fewer administrative processes, fewer opportunities to make human errors, and increased operational consistency. The system offers centralized dashboards that present the current compliance data, trace the number of exceptions, present the current remediation work, and indicate the changes in drift patterns.

With the help of governance processes, organizations enjoy higher compliance monitoring as it employs automation as long as they are conducting their business.

3.5.9 Strategic Implications and Organizational Resilience

Active compliance enables organizations to have governance where exception handling and compliance drift management make up a novel operational governance mechanism. Exception management process also allows organizations to manage their operational needs in accordance with the set process as they meet their duty of ensuring transparency in operations. The organization manages the operational standards by managing drifts that puts effective controls of their system to prevent entry of threats of technological systems into their working environment. Organizations that institutionalize both practices experience four advantages which include reduced regulatory exposure and improved operational stability and enhanced cybersecurity posture and stronger audit defensibility. The organizations create a governance culture which allows them to use both agile processes and accountable practices. Organizations require additional resources beyond their current auditing and control systems to achieve compliance with contemporary technological requirements. The system requires two components for successful operation which include active control of all deviations and full protection of its system configuration. Organizations establish permanent compliance systems through exception handling and drift management which allow them to handle regulatory changes while meeting their legal responsibilities and preserving public confidence.

Multiple Choice Questions (MCQs)

1. **What is the primary purpose of Policy-as-Code (PaC)?**
   A. To manually document organizational policies
   B. To embed compliance rules into automated systems
   C. To eliminate the need for governance teams
   D. To reduce cloud infrastructure costs

2. **Which tool is commonly used for implementing Policy-as-Code in cloud environments?**
   E. Microsoft Excel
   F. GitHub
   G. Open Policy Agent
   H. Adobe Photoshop

3. **Infrastructure as Code (IaC) helps compliance by:**
   A. Allowing random configuration changes
   B. Ensuring consistent and repeatable infrastructure deployments
   C. Removing the need for audits
   D. Disabling version control

4. **Which of the following is a key benefit of Infrastructure as Code for compliance consistency?**
   A. Increased human intervention
   B. Reduced visibility of infrastructure
   C. Version-controlled infrastructure configurations
   D. Manual approval for every deployment

5. **What is the best practice for managing secrets and credentials in automated environments?**
   A. Hardcoding them in application source code
   B. Storing them in public repositories
   C. Using a secure vault service
   D. Sharing them via email
6. **Which tool is widely used for secure secrets management?**
   A. Notepad
   B. Hashi Corp Vault
   C. Microsoft Paint
   D. Calculator
7. **Continuous compliance monitoring primarily ensures:**
   A. One-time policy verification
   B. Compliance only during audits
   C. Ongoing validation of security and regulatory requirements
   D. Elimination of security controls
8. **What is compliance drift?**
   A. Automatic correction of policy violations
   B. Gradual deviation of systems from approved configurations
   C. Rapid deployment of infrastructure
   D. Complete removal of security rules
9. **Exception handling in compliance management should:**
   A. Ignore minor violations
   B. Be undocumented
   C. Follow a formal approval and tracking process
   D. Be applied permanently without review

10. **Which approach best helps prevent compliance drift?**
    A. Manual spot-checking once a year
    B. Disabling automated alerts
    C. Automated monitoring and remediation
    D. Allowing unrestricted administrator access

Answers

1	2	3	4	5	6	7	8	9	10
B	C	B	C	C	B	C	B	C	C

Chapter 4
Audit Readiness and Governance in DevOps

4.1 LOGGING, MONITORING, AND EVIDENCE COLLECTION

The main functional foundation of the audit readiness and governance assurance within the DevOps-oriented organizations is the logging and monitoring, as well as the evidence gathering. As the system moves to a software delivery model, driven by continuous integration and continuous delivery (CI/CD), the amount, speed, and quantity of data generated by the system only increase exponentially. In each code commit, infrastructure change, and deployment activity, configuration change, and user access event, digital traces are created. With proper management, such traces will create formal records that will reveal the efficiency of control, adherence to the rules and responsibility by the organization. The changing systems have high rate of loss of visibility in devops environments in the absence of any structure in logging and systematic monitoring of these systems leading to weak governance structures.

The manual documentation that included change request forms and post-facto gathering of evidences within the audit cycles was a big part of the traditional IT governance models. DevOps on the contrary is all about automation, speed and continuous improvement. This transition needs an equally computerized and constant form of governance. The events occurring during operations are logged and analyzed in a real time like fashion through monitoring and formalized into a limited number of artifacts as evidence. These mechanisms comprise a clear traceable structure of record that enables agility in technical operation as well as regulation and tactical command.

The importance of quality evidence in a highly controlled sphere cannot be overestimated in case of highly regulated industries such as the financial sector, health services, telecom services and institutions of the public. The auditors are making the organizations to put bigger demand on them not only to show the documented policies but also to show verifiable evidence that the controls are working in reality. Consequently, logging and monitoring methods ought to be made not to bother with the operations but to confirm governance, carry out a forensic audit and guarantee adherence over the long-term (Taneja, 2024).

4.1.1 Logging as the Foundation of Governance and Traceability

Logging is a process that is used to categorize the events generated by the applications, the elements of the infrastructure, the security controls, as well as the pipeline of delivery. DevOps ecosystems produce logs at a number of levels: application logs that capture the runtime behavior; system logs that capture the operating system events; infrastructure logs that capture the provisioning and configuration change events; access logs that capture the authentication and authorization events; and the CI/CD logs that capture the code integration and deployment events. Containerized and cloud-based architecture introduces a lot of complexity to logging. On platforms such as Kubernetes that organize dynamic clusters, containers can be destroyed and re-created in just a few seconds. Similarly, the Docker environments offer secluded container-based run-time logs. The nature of these elements is temporary, and hence logs ought to be captured and centralized before termination so that websites are not left without data. It is possible that the lack of the ability to implement centralized logging in those environments results in incomplete audit trails.

There is yet another aspect of logging that CI/CD pipelines introduce that is very critical. Server automation tools such as Jenkins and code repositories such as GitHub generate detailed records of code changes, merge requests, build runs, automated test results, artifact generation, and deployment claims. The individual developer's traceability to the production releases is provided in the logs.

This traceability aids accountability, non-repudiation, and segregation of duties in the governance aspect. Logs should meet certain integrity requirements in order to be used as reliable audit evidence. Timestamp synchronization between systems assures chronological correctness, unchangeability by non-authorized persons, secrecy by encryption, and preservation by retention policies ensure that the data is available at all times during regulating periods. Governance structures must specify ownership of logs, storage criteria, and archiving procedures. Audits and legal proceedings cannot accept logs that have no integrity controls as a defense in a court of law.

4.1.2 Monitoring as Continuous Oversight and Control Validation

Where logging documents the events, monitoring interprets and analyzes events with predefined rules, thresholds, and compliance requirements. Monitoring systems are systems that consolidate the log information, correlate activities in distributed environments, identify abnormalities, and issue alerts in the event of deviations. In terms of governance, tracking converts the nonliving records to the observational living records. Splunk, Elastic Stack, and Microsoft Sentinel are centralized data-aggregating monitoring platforms that offer live dashboards, analysis functions to combine application, infrastructure, and security device data, as well as cloud services logs. These systems help organizations to show that there are controls that are being implemented and not just written.

Constant observation promotes various governance goals. It ensures access controls are functional, deployed workflows are approved, unauthorized changes to configuration are detected, and that security patches are implemented within a stipulated period. Monitoring dashboards and alert histories in an audit situation are used as evidence of continuous monitoring and prompt reaction to the events. Instead of rushing to gather evidence by the conclusion of an audit period, those organizations that have well-matured monitoring capacity are capable of delivering real-time compliance snapshots. Nevertheless, the successful monitoring is to be carefully calibrated. Too many alerts can cause fatigue, making one less responsive, whereas too few can cause activities that are not compliant to go unnoticed. Government systems should thus put in place risk-based monitoring measures that are consistent with organizational priorities and regulatory risks.

4.1.3 Evidence Collection Across the DevOps Lifecycle

Evidence is captured not only based on raw logs, but it is also captured in the form of structured artifacts that are created during the software development lifecycle. Some of the evidence in DevOps settings can be source code commit logs, peer approval logs, automated tests logs, artifacts of a build, infrastructure as code (IAC) scripts, deployment artifacts, vulnerability testing, and rollback logs. The verifiable documentation is created at every stage of the CI/CD pipeline. As an example, a commit identifier identifies a particular change in the code to a developer; a pull request history proves the presence of peer reviews and approvals; automated test reports validate quality checks, and deployment records confirm controlled releases. A combination of these artifacts to form an overall audit trail is possible when they are automatically captured and indexed.

Evidence collection has an important role in automation. Documentation processes are likely to be inconsistent and subject to human error, especially in environments in which the DevOps processes are very high. Evidence is captured automatically and is complete and less administrative. Also, the connection between CI/CD systems and governance, risk, and compliance (GRC) tools makes it possible to structure artifact mapping to the control requirements. Evidence is also enhanced by the use of secure storage mechanisms. Hash, digital signatures, encryption both in the rest and in transit, as well as role-based access controls, are some of the techniques that eliminate tampering and unauthorized access. The retirement schedules should be in accordance with the regulatory requirements, agreement, and internal policies. Organizations can integrate evidence gathering into pipeline operations to develop a state of continuous audit preparedness instead of periodic compliance preparation.

4.1.4 Centralization, SIEM Integration, and Multi-Cloud Considerations

Contemporary businesses are often run in hybrid and multi-cloud settings. Examples of cloud services decomposing infrastructure events, access logs, and configuration changes into native logging services include Amazon Web Services, Microsoft Azure, and Google Cloud. Nevertheless, the use of isolated provider-specific logs can lead to a problem of fragmented visibility.

The concept of centralized log management ensures that logs of various origins are distributed into a single repository. Security Information and Event Management (SIEM) integration enhances cross-system correlation that helps in the management of on-premise systems, containers, and cloud workloads, and services provided by third parties in a holistic manner. The centralization renders the process of preparing audits less difficult as it provides a spot of truth in terms of compliance.

Multi-cloud designs, however, introduce complexity in log normalization, consistency of retention, and compliance with data sovereignty. The governance teams should ensure that they have standardized forms of logs, time settings, and that all environments must share an identical retention policy. Ownership models and documented escalation processes are other boosters of oversight mechanisms.

4.1.5 Governance Controls: Integrity, Segregation, and Chain of Custody

To survive scrutiny by auditors, organizations should adopt governance controls that can guarantee the integrity of evidence and that they are accountable. Role-based access control can be used to prevent changes because the person cannot be involved in the implementation of the change or granting of the changes; the person can be denied the opportunity to change the log repository; and the approval workflow is documented, which is used to create a transparent decision-making process. Chain-of-custody procedures record the procedures of evidence collection, storage, access, and archives. Attempts of access also must be logged, forming meta-evidence to strengthen transparency. Cryptographic hashing of records periodically can be used to verify that the records stored are not altered. Encryption protects confidentiality, especially in controlled sectors that deal with sensitive information. The level of responsibility of log management, monitoring, and retention of evidence should be clearly defined in governance documentation. Even technically sound logging systems cannot be expected to comply satisfactorily without specific accountability structures.

4.1.6 Challenges and Strategic Considerations

Logging and monitoring systems have operational and strategic issues, even though they are important. Large volumes of logs raise the expense of storage and processing. There are temporary infrastructure elements that can produce temporary logs that need to be aggregated quickly. Logs in different formats make it difficult to correlate. The laws on data privacy provide limitations on the storage of personally identifiable data in logs. To overcome these troubles, organizations need to implement scalable architectures and standard logging frameworks. Risk-based retention policies can balance the compliance requirements and storage efficiency. The effectiveness should be monitored periodically, and with the new threats or regulatory changes to the continuous improvement procedures, the thresholds should be adjusted. Neither should logging nor gathering of evidence be regarded as a compliance overhead, but as bases of organizational resilience as a strategic offset. Complete visibility enables response to the incident, develops stakeholders' trust, and maximizes operational visibility.

The governance infrastructure of DevOps settings consists of logging, evidence monitoring, and collection. When implemented adequately as part of the CI/CD pipelines and cloud system, they offer an automated and continuous recording of the activities in the organization. Through the record, it is possible to have transparent control over it, react promptly to incidents, and have defensible audit trails that are unresponsive to regulatory scrutiny. As the world continues to become digitized and regulations become more and more pressing, organizations must be ready to move beyond reactive audit preparation into embedded compliance capabilities. The revenue logging and monitoring systems installed instill mature structures that translate operational information into strategic governance resources in a manner that does not affect speed and agility at the expense of accountability. Finally, the effectiveness of the DevOps governance model within an organization is identified in its capability to generate credible, tamper-resistant evidence proving the effectiveness of control and its maintenance.

4.2 AUDIT REQUIREMENTS IN CONTINUOUS DELIVERY ENVIRONMENTS

The fast development of the Agile methodology and Continuous Delivery (CD) practices has radically changed the process of software systems development, deployment, and maintenance. The contemporary DevOps setting is marked by the rapid rate of deployment, automated pipelines, the use of Infrastructure as Code (IaC), micro-services architecture, and widespread use of clouds. System configurations, application logic, and infrastructure components may vary several times a day in such environments. This dynamic environment puts into question the traditional governance and audit models, which are made to be relatively stable in an IT environment. Traditionally, audits were done once a year or semi-annually based on the collection of retrospective evidence and the use of manual validation of controls. Although this model was sufficient in the case of a static IT landscape, it can no longer be used as a guarantee in the Continuous Delivery environments. The one-year audit cycle is inadequate to guarantee that the security controls were in effect when the system changes were of high and high frequency. As a result, an additional audit paradigm is required, which would be up to the speed, automation, and complexity of DevOps required in organizations. Continuous Auditing is a new governance requirement brought about by the change.

4.2.1 Limitations of Traditional Audit Cycles in DevOps Environments

A variety of structural constraints are imposed on Continuous Delivery situations by conventional methods of audit as well:

- **Retrospective Validation -** Controls are not being tested on time, and at most, they do not occur until months after the occurrence of changes in the system. This delay influences the ability to detect and correct risks as quickly as possible.
- **Periodic Evidence Collection -** Evidence is not gathered continuously but in impregnable periods, which create blind spots between the audit periods.
- **Manual Processes -** Manual processes are common in evidence collection, validation, and reporting, which are inefficient and error-prone in dynamically changing systems.
- **High Audit Disruption -** Every year, audits have been known to disrupt operations significantly due to the fact that they are obliged to spend enormous amounts of resources on documentation to demonstrate to them that they were keeping up.

These limitations affect the quality of assurance within the context of the incremental and continuous DevOps environments. It is impossible to reduce adherence to periodic system state check points. Instead, audit economies are to be close to real-time (Jain, 2024).

4.2.2 The Need for Continuous Monitoring and Real-Time Evidence

Continuous Delivery environments need audit processes that run concurrently with the development and operations processes. Each code commit, infrastructure modification, update to configuration, or deployment presents an opportunity for risk. As such, security controls need to be verified on an ongoing basis, as opposed to periodically.

Constant surveillance is to see that:

- Configuration baselines are maintained.
- Access controls remain properly enforced.
- Security vulnerabilities are detected early.
- Policy violations are identified immediately.

Continuous monitoring becomes the foundation for Continuous Auditing. Whereas in monitoring, attention is given to operational visibility, Continuous Auditing provides a formal check of the effectiveness of controls. They work together in offering long-term audit preparedness as opposed to short-term compliance at audit instance.

4.2.3 Increasing Audit Frequency: An Incremental Improvement

The first reaction to quick change is to raise the frequency of audits, such as quarterly or monthly audits, rather than annual audits. This method will decrease the difference between the cycles of control validation and enhance the response to the exposure to risks.

Nevertheless, the problem cannot be completely solved by increasing frequency. Monthly audits might be inadequate even in environments where there are several deployments every day. Moreover, the cost and resource requirements are also very large due to the increased frequency of audits. Thus, as much as it can be an interim measure, more audit frequency is to be found to be accompanied by automation and integration into the CI/CD pipeline.

4.2.4 Security by Design in Continuous Delivery

A better solution would be to incorporate security controls as part of the system lifecycle, also known as Security by Design. Instead of identifying failure of control after being deployed, the controls are being proactively incorporated in the development, testing, deployment, and operational processes.

Security by Design guarantees that:

- Secure coding practices are enforced automatically.

- Authentication and authorization mechanisms are built into the application architecture.
- Infrastructure configurations are defined through secure templates.
- Automated security testing is embedded in CI/CD pipelines.

This approach reduces reliance on after-the-fact validation and shifts governance left in the development lifecycle. It is very similar to DevSecOps, which implies automated security controls and constant validation of them as part of the pipeline workflow.

4.2.5 Continuous Auditing as a Governance Model

Continuous Auditing extends continuous monitoring by automating the verification of control effectiveness. It involves the systematic, real-time collection and evaluation of control evidence from all managed components within an information system.

In Continuous Delivery environments, this includes:

- Infrastructure components (servers, networks, cloud resources)
- System software (operating systems, databases)
- Application components (business logic, APIs)
- CI/CD pipeline configurations
- Identity and access management systems

Continuous Auditing ensures that deviations from policy are detected immediately rather than during periodic reviews.

4.2.6 Architectural Components of Continuous Auditing

A successful Continuous Auditing system usually has a number of built-in elements:

- **Managed Objects**

  Managed objects are all the infrastructure and objects of the application that are involved in the delivery of services. Every managed object should be able to provide quantifiable properties of interest to the security-related controls, including configuration, access, and patching.

- **Control Evidence Export**

  Control evidence is produced by each delivered object that proves the efficiency of the controls employed. Evidence can be in the form of system logs, configuration files, authentication records, or vulnerability scan findings. Structured logs are examples of standardized formats, which are analyzed automatically.

- **Control Database**

  Business rules and compliance requirements are kept in a centralized control database. These policies establish acceptable setups and anticipated behaviors. The control can be based on ISO 27001 standards or even an internal security policy.

- **Control Evidence Repository**

  Gathered evidence is centralized and normalized to be consistent. This warehouse allows tracking and analyzing the effectiveness of controls in the past.

- **Continuous Auditing Engine**

  Control evidence is automatically compared to the set rules in the auditing engine. Deviations are identified and alert is raised, and a corrective workflow can be initiated.

- **Audit Dashboard**

  Control effectiveness is represented in the visual of a real-time dashboard in terms of systems, services, and compliance areas. This provides transparency and facilitates management control.

4.2.7 Cloud and Third-Party Challenges

In the current Continuous Delivery setup, the use of cloud applications and third-party solutions is common. These services can be black-box services, where fewer of the underlying infrastructure controls are visible.

Although service-level agreements (SLAs) and certification (i.e., ISO 27001 or ISAE 3402) offer a certain degree of assurance, organizations still have a role to play in assessing the legitimacy of security controls in the framework of their operations. Continuous Auditing should hence include:

- Vendor risk assessments
- Review of third-party audit reports
- API-based evidence extraction where available
- Monitoring of shared responsibility controls

Cloud adoption increases complexity but does not eliminate accountability.

4.2.8 Challenges in Implementing Continuous Auditing

Continuous Auditing has its virtues, and there exist work issues:

- **Skill Requirements**

  Cybersecurity expertise, DevOps engineering expertise, automation skills, and auditing expertise are the required skills and experience required to perform continuous Auditing. The majority of the organizations lack individuals qualified in the compliance structures and technical pipe constructions. Sometimes there is a need to fill this void by training, acquiring certain talent, and encouraging inter-functional collaboration.

- **Evidence Availability**

  Continuous Auditing is based on evidence collection in the form of automation and real-time, as supported by system and application-based evidence. However, the implemented log exports or the extraction of data in the form of API may not be compatible with legacy systems and some third-party platforms. The outcome of this constraint is the possibility of manual interventions, which will lead to an inefficient and unreliable process of auditing.

- **Control Mapping**

  The transfer of high-level compliance standards to technical controls, which are testable, is a complex procedure. The under control objectives should be subjected to some control validations based on the degree of exposure to risks. Clarity gaps in mappings could result in coverage gaps or recurring control reviews.

- **Centralization Risks**

  Continuous auditing solutions bring together sensitive compliance and security data in centralized repositories. Such a concentration of information, however, unless secured, can be a prime target of the attackers. The audit infrastructure should be put in place with high levels of access control, encryption, and monitoring to avoid unauthorized access to the infrastructure.

- **Cost and Complexity**

  Constant Auditing needs tools, system integrations, and process redesign investment. Organizations are forced to incur expenses on automation platforms, logging systems, dashboards, and maintenance. The technical and organizational complexity can be significant, especially within a big or highly regulated environment.

4.2.9 Governance Implications

Continued Auditing changes governance into an active, built-in process of reaction instead of an event-driven approach. It supports:

- Continuous compliance
- Reduced audit disruption

- Faster remediation cycles
- Enhanced transparency
- Sustained audit readiness

The adoption of Continuous Delivery by organizations requires alignment of governance structures with automated control validation systems. Audit requirements are not a point of control anymore, but inherent features in digital operations.

Clearly, the audit requirements within the Continuous Delivery environment demand that the organization change the current approach of undertaking regular assessments that evaluate their systems at previous periods, to a new system that will offer ongoing assessments by automated testing. The fast-paced DevOps ecosystem dictates that the frequency of audits should be higher than that which is currently practiced by the organization, since the annual audits that are currently in use in the organization do not provide the confidence that they need. To achieve full compliance, the organizations must have security controls throughout their development process, along with Continuous Auditing systems as part of their governance requirements, to ensure that their development process is fully compliant. Organizations can achieve compliance by using Security by Design principles together with automated evidence collection and real-time control validation, which allows them to maintain their DevOps operational pace. Continuous Auditing needs to become a strategic development that organizations require for their digital governance needs because it creates both technical and organizational implementation barriers.

4.3 CHANGE MANAGEMENT AND APPROVAL WORKFLOWS

The DevOps approach keeps organizations in a state of constant transformation. The system experiences multiple daily updates that include application releases, infrastructure changes, configuration updates, security vulnerability fixes, documentation updates, and service improvement activities. The Continuous Delivery method allows organizations to deliver new products at a faster pace, but introduces potential threats to system stability, security protection, and regulatory compliance that require proper change control procedures. Structured change management processes, together with approval workflows, establish a framework that enables organizations to achieve both agile operational efficiency and effective control capabilities. The change management framework establishes procedures to record all changes from their initial assessment through to final approval and subsequent implementation and execution of the planned modifications. Organizations need adaptive governance systems to manage their rapid deployment challenges because DevOps environments differ from traditional IT systems that depended on centralized common changes. The objective is to slow down the process of innovation because the organization needs to confirm that all changes meet its business objectives, risk tolerance levels, and compliance standards. The approval process design minimizes service interruptions while maintaining operational efficiency and building trust with all parties involved. (Mainville, 2023).

4.3.1 Importance of Controlled Change in DevOps

Organizations that need to control changes in their IT systems face challenges because these systems support their business operations and financial activities and serve their customers. Changes that organizations do not manage properly or review adequately lead to four major consequences, which include service outages, data breaches, regulatory violations, and damage to their public image. All modifications that involve hardware changes, application code updates, infrastructure configuration alterations, or documentation updates must proceed through established procedures.

The change management system of an organization provides three essential functions, which include establishing consistent procedures, delivering visible information, and creating responsibility systems. The system enables organizations to adapt to new business requirements while protecting existing system functions and stopping recurring problems through its ability to reduce work duplication. The structured approval process in cloud environments and distributed systems decreases the chance of unintentional system failures, which occur when one system fails and causes other systems to fail.

4.3.2 Risk-Based Change Classification

Different kinds of changes present different levels of risk. The modern principle of change governance requires organizations to classify their changes according to their impact and their complexity. The system divides changes into seven categories, which include minor changes, normal changes, significant changes, major changes, pre-approved changes, expedited changes, and emergency changes. The classification defines what level of examination and permission needs to be obtained.

The process requires organizations to conduct complete risk evaluations, which need to obtain official consent from their top management for all high-risk changes that involve altering fundamental systems, network security settings, and essential business software. Organizations use simpler operational procedures to handle low-risk changes because this method helps them work more effectively. Organizations achieve their goals of timely approvals through risk-based processes, which help them maintain control over changes that have the potential to disrupt service operations and regulatory compliance.

4.3.3 Roles and Responsibilities (Change Manager, CAB, ECAB)

The establishment of particular role definitions helps organizations to boost their accountability throughout their change management processes. The Change Advisory Board (CAB) performs its main governance function through its assessment and authorization process of changes that will create significant effects. The group typically consists of members who represent development, operations, security, help desk management, business units, and third-party vendors who are applicable to the situation. The CAB needs to assess three elements, which include potential risks and business impact, and strategic objective alignment, before it can grant approval. The Emergency Change Advisory Board (ECAB) functions to handle urgent situations that demand immediate decision-making. The process supports critical incident resolution because it allows access to vital systems while maintaining necessary governance controls. The Change Manager oversees all aspects of the change management process. The responsibilities involve preparing and validating change tickets, communicating procedures, organizing review meetings, compiling key metrics, ensuring documentation completeness, and obtaining formal sign-offs. The Change Manager acts as the primary authority who manages all aspects of process control and documentation traceability.

4.3.4 Ticket-Based Workflow Governance

Organizations use structured ticketing systems as the main requirement for their current change approval processes. The change request process requires all requests to be documented and tracked through established stages that begin with submission, continue through assessment and prioritization, testing and approval, implementation, and post-implementation review. The ticketing systems store all essential data, which includes risk evaluations, implementation schedules, rollback procedures, and communication documentation. The system permits organizations to monitor all dependencies that exist between their connected changes while they keep their documentation tracking and their access control through role-based user permissions. The systems provide better transparency while they create approved records, and they produce auditable documents that help organizations meet compliance standards. Ticket-based systems create a complete digital record of all activities, which enables teams to have better accountability while they work together.

4.3.5 Emergency and Expedited Changes

The need for structured workflows does not erase the requirement that change management systems must handle emergency situations. Immediate changes become essential when organizations need to restore operations, fix security problems, or protect their essential business activities. Organizations create specific rules to determine which situations qualify as emergencies because they want to stop people from abusing their system for fast-tracking emergency requests. The ECAB evaluates emergency changes, but all aspects of the change must be recorded even when approval occurs quickly. The organization conducts post-implementation reviews to evaluate the process effectiveness, confirm results, and determine which lessons should be learned. The system establishes a method to handle emergencies while maintaining strict rules for operational control.

4.3.6 Back-Out and Recovery Planning

Every change proposal needs to present an unambiguous back-out plan that defines how to reverse changes from the proposal. Back-out plans provide step-by-step instructions for reversing a change if it fails or produces unintended consequences. The success criteria establishment process specifies responsible individuals who will implement recovery procedures. Organizations achieve operational continuity through their recovery planning process, which protects their financial and corporate reputation from potential service disruptions. Organizations can increase their operational resilience by preparing for potential failure situations, while their failed changes can be restored to normal operations through efficient processes that cause minimal disturbance.

4.3.7 Automation vs Human Oversight

The use of automation improves both the operational performance and capacity expansion capabilities of change management processes, which DevOps teams implement. The system carries out automated ticket routing alongside approval notification, triggering escalation and status update, and monitoring tools integration that assists in reducing the amount of administrative work and facilitating quicker processing. The system places too much reliance on automated procedures that makes it difficult to control effectively. Humans are supposed to make decisions on critical issues that involve accepting massive changes in infrastructure and giving remote access and authorization for significant software installation. A mixed strategy should be adopted in organizations, automating the basic processes, but needing the assistance of human professionals in handling the most important business processes. The hybrid system allows organizations to retain accountability for their actions and, at the same time, be in a position to respond fast to evolving circumstances.

4.3.8 Continuous Improvement in Change Governance

The continuous improvement in change governance focuses on transformation within an organization aimed at delivering value to stakeholders and clients. <|human|>The continuous improvement in change governance is concerned with change in an organization that is bound to provide value to the stakeholders and clients.

Implementation of change management needs to be continuous since the process demands that organizations build systems that run on well-established procedures to evaluate processes. The organization must come up with a Process Improvement Program that will help them to evaluate the efficiency of workflow by undertaking systematic assessments. The performance metrics utilized in the organization are the incident frequency, change success rates, rollback incident approvals, turnaround times, and service downtimes that are used to gauge the efficiency of the processes. As it enhances its operation processes and response capacity, the organization uses regular assessments to uncover the bottlenecks and eliminate redundant approval routes as it works on its improvement processes. Continuous improvement is applied to organizations to ensure the systems of governance are maintained, as they must align with the latest technological advancements, new legal requirements, and business strategies.

4.3.9 Integration with Audit and Compliance

The implementation of change management processes establishes essential requirements for conducting audits and meeting regulatory standards. The process of change approval results in created documents, which include permission records, risk evaluations, testing documentation, implementation records, and assessment results. The established records function as evidence that controls work effectively during both internal audits and external audits. The organization maintains proper accountability through its formal governance systems, which include CAB oversight, established approval processes, and documented escalation methods and access rights assigned to specific positions. Organizations enhance their capacity to meet regulatory requirements by creating change management processes that follow established governance structures and business requirements.

The governance processes of DevOps and Continuous Delivery systems depend on Change Management and Approval Workflows as their core element. Unregulated modifications to modern IT operations, which require organizations to adopt new technologies and perform multiple system updates, create significant dangers that affect operational performance, system protection, and regulatory compliance. The combination of risk-based classification with established roles and ticket-based governance systems, emergency controls, and structured rollback planning and ongoing improvement mechanisms enables organizations to maintain control of their operations while maintaining their ability to respond quickly. The application of effective change management procedures together with auditing and compliance systems establishes complete traceability and responsibility, which helps organizations maintain stable operational functions. The structured approval workflows help organizations achieve fast value delivery while they maintain their governance frameworks and reduce their risk in fast-changing digital environments.

4.4 PREPARING FOR INTERNAL AND EXTERNAL AUDITS

Organizations need to establish an auditing framework that combines structured methods with active monitoring systems through technological tools to ensure their operational activities meet audit requirements. Organizations with conventional structures developed their auditing processes through regular activities that started when the auditing process began. DevOps-driven enterprises that use cloud-native infrastructure and automated CI/CD pipelines need organizations to create their audit processes through active work. Organizations need to create systems that enable their daily activities to become audit-ready through operational procedures, control systems, and governance frameworks. Continuous governance requires organizations to perform compliance checks and control validation procedures at the same time they develop new software. Organizations prepare for audits through effective audit preparation, which decreases operational work during the audit process while improving internal control systems and operational visibility and building trust with stakeholders. Organizations need to view audits as governance maturity assessment tools instead of external inspections, which show their lack of operational control. Modern enterprises operate in highly dynamic environments where configuration changes, code deployments, and infrastructure modifications occur frequently. Organizations need to provide authentic documentation that shows their control systems function properly and that they manage risks and meet regulatory standards in their operations. The audit preparation process involves the organization to put governance-based systems that process risk assessment, along with documentation and evaluation of internal controls, and preparation of their cultural aspects to be monitored immediately. The following subsections discuss the key factors that contribute to effective audit procedures of the continuous governance systems (McCarty, 2024).

4.4.1 Establishing an Audit-Ready Governance Structure

The audit preparation begins with the organization's developing an inclusive governance framework, which they ensure they document in detail. The governance system processes are the foundation that must be prepared to mitigate audit assessments by the organizations. Organizations should develop entire sets of policies and principles and regulate objectives that should align with their corporate objectives and with the norms that are demanded by various regulations and industry rules. The records need to be used and evaluated frequently to be implemented successfully. The governance documentation must set certain departmental responsibilities that must consist of control systems, permission systems, and methods of escalation. DevOps environments demand organizations create accountability among development teams, operations teams, security teams, and compliance teams. The control ownership system allows auditors to track the ownership of the control to the specific persons who are using the control system to track the accountability process. An organization needs an audit-ready governance system that includes control frameworks that map directly to its specific operational risks. The organization needs to create links between change management controls and operational risk mitigation, access control policies, data protection risks, incident response procedures, and cybersecurity resilience. The organization needs to establish its infrastructure-as-code standards and CI/CD pipeline controls documentation because this shows how its automated systems execute governance rules throughout their processes. The presence of executive oversight creates greater audit readiness for organizations. The senior management team and the audit committee need to participate actively in their respective roles because this shows their organization's commitment to maintaining transparency and following compliance rules. The leadership team needs to support audit preparation activities because this will help the organization to incorporate these processes into its strategic planning activities. The presence of executive sponsors will establish governance authority that maintains control throughout the organization.

4.4.2 Risk Assessment and Audit Planning

The process of risk assessment establishes the essential foundation that auditors need to properly prepare their work. Organizations must conduct regular evaluations of their financial, operational, technological, and regulatory risks to establish their audit priorities. The risk assessment procedure provides auditors with a structured method to determine their resource distribution, which leads to optimal results for organizational stability and compliance requirements. Organizations use enterprise-wide risk assessments to create their internal audit plans. Organizations will focus on high-risk areas, which include privileged access management, third-party vendor controls, change governance and data privacy protections, and cloud configuration security. The risk-based approach enhances the efficiency of the audits as it focuses on the key security vulnerabilities as opposed to assessing the trivial security threats.

The preparation of the external audit must be in line with the standards of the relevant regulations or industry. Organizations must understand both compliance requirements and internal controls in order to have a successful evaluation. The audit findings will occur in the existence of internal control documents that are not in accordance with regulatory standards. Companies with continuous governance activities have to analyze their risks using a risk assessment that is based on technology. Systemic vulnerabilities are caused by the presence of automation-related vulnerabilities, pipeline misconfigurations, a lack of logging, unauthorized deployments, and segregation of duties conflicts in organizations. Those organizations that are proactive in detecting and preventing these risks will have higher audit outcomes that demonstrate their high governance skills.

4.4.3 Documentation and Evidence Management

One of the most crucial aspects that the auditors must prepare their work with is documentation and evidence management. Documentary evidence is the main tool of auditors to evaluate the functionality of the controls and the functioning of the operational processes. Organizations must develop correct records that are inclusive of all the necessary information in order to facilitate their governance endeavors. Organizations ought to develop formal documentation that comprises their policies, procedures, control narratives, system diagrams, workflow descriptions, and document versioning control. Organizations that are guided by the DevOps principles must ensure that their documentation contains all automated processes that involve their CI / CD pipeline infrastructure provisioning scripts, access control systems, and deployment approval processes.

Continuous governance environments through the introduction of automated evidence collection tools introduce significant change to audit processes. Logs that are generated by the system, along with configuration baselines, deployment histories, access review reports, and ticketing system records, provide objective evidence on the way controls are functioning. The continuous monitoring tools have the ability of generating real time boards that display compliance with the set policies. Evidence management systems combined with centralized repositories of documentation make auditing easier for an organization. Effective evidence retrieval can be achieved through proper indexing and standardized naming conventions, as well as retention schedules and access controls, to safeguard the integrity of data. Companies that have systematic evidence management systems have quicker audits and are showing greater governance abilities.

4.4.4 Pre-Audit Internal Control Validation

To ascertain their preparedness for their future audit work, the organizations are required to conduct the internal control tests by using their internal control testing or conducting their mock audit testing. The preparatory assessment tests will help to know whether the controls are formulated correctly and whether they are operating as planned in the actual operations. Preventive measures can be made by the management team since they can detect the problems with control before the official audit evaluations begin. The control validation process must ensure that the design strength as well as the operational capability of the system is valid. The approved processes of change recorded should have traceable approval processes, which are stored through the ticketing systems. The organizations have to submit evidence of their access review policies in terms of documentation that they had performed their periodic reviews and traced their procedure of correcting the identified problems. The incident response plans need to provide evidence through documented investigation methods and their procedures for reporting incidents after they occur.

The validation process which occurs before audits begins relies heavily on automated systems. The continuous monitoring systems for compliance can detect changes in system configuration which should not happen and trace unapproved modifications and monitor breaks in security protocols at the moment they occur. The organizations use automated notifications to solve problems before they become official audit issues. The process of verifying controls which occurs before the audit improves control effectiveness and decreases risks related to reputation and regulations.

4.4.5 Preparing for Internal Audits

The organization conducts internal audits throughout the entire year according to its risk-based audit plan. The process of internal audit preparation requires teams to establish audit boundaries which they must learn who will handle their duties and all necessary documents must be ready at the time of their request. The departments under evaluation must establish dedicated audit contacts who will handle all communication needs and document requirements for the audit process.

The employees are supposed to view internal audits as organizational development tools rather than seeing these audits as a compulsory requirement. The internal auditors provide unbiased evaluations that assist organizations to improve their business operations and risk management practices and their governance frameworks. The collaboration of the management and audit teams is crucial since such cooperation creates an environment of open interaction and the beneficial cooperation.

Tracking remediation is a crucial component that is required in preparing the internal audit operations. The organization should come up with detailed records of their corrective action plans that should contain specific work and time of completion. The regular monitoring system that the organization puts in place will determine its commitment to continuous development that prepares the organization to the future external evaluation procedures.

4.4.6 Preparing for External Audits

External audits should be formally coordinated because it has regulatory, contractual and reputational consequences. The start point is to make sure that the scope of audit, timelines and documentation requirements is agreed upon with the external audit team. Close integration of finance, IT, compliance, and legal departments makes sure that the preparation is done comprehensively.

Companies that undergo compliance-based auditing, including those corresponding to the Health Insurance Portability and Accountability Act, Payment Card Industry Data Security Standard, ISO/IEC 27001:2022, Federal Risk and Authorization management Program, or Cybersecurity Maturity Model Certification, need to make sure that internal controls are accurately aligned with regulatory standards.

Comparisons between internal documentation and compliance requirements will make it easy to review by the auditor and minimize the chances of material findings. Companies are advised to do preparedness tests before the actual engagement to ensure documentation and other evidence are in place.

In external audits, proper and frequent communication is vital. The evidence-based answers should be presented by special representatives who would be backed with the artifacts. Lack of order in documentation or lack of consistency in explanations can cast a dark cloud on the reliability of governance and effectiveness of internal controls.

4.4.7 Training, Awareness, and Cultural Readiness

Preparation of audits is not just a technical control and documentation task but the organizations culture that will appreciate compliance and accountability. The employees have to be informed on their roles in ensuring control effectiveness and assistance in audit.

Data protection policies, access control duties, secure coding policy, incident reporting, and change approval policy should be covered at regular training programs. Awareness of compliance in the development and operation processes of DevOps would guarantee the application of governance principles.

Cultural preparedness helps with the resistance in bank audit engagements and increases collaborative involvement. Once compliance is integrated into the day-to-day activities, audit preparation will cease being a reactive requirement and become a standard governmental activity. Ongoing learning and sensitization will result in sustainable compliance maturity.

The readiness to the internal and external audits in the continuously governed situation presupposes the organization of the governance structure, the thorough assessment of risks, the disciplined practice of documentation, the active control validation, and the cultural consideration. Internal audits focus on the continuous improvement and operational improvement, and the external audit gives the independent certification to the regulators, investors, customers, and other stakeholders.

Audit preparedness in DevOps-oriented companies should be part of automated deployment pipelines, real-time evidence collection and monitoring mechanisms, and continuous monitoring systems. Companies that incorporate audit preparations within the normal running of operations record a higher level of governance maturity, transparency and resilience during regulatory audit process. Finally, audit preparation in advance can convert compliance into a regular task into a tactical element of sustainable business administration.

4.5 ROLE-BASED ACCESS CONTROL AND SEGREGATION OF DUTIES

Access management in the contemporary DevOps-led business is no longer an edge activity IT service, but a centralized system of governance that has a direct impact on compliance posture, operational resilience, and audit preparedness. With pipelines growing faster and infrastructure programmable, companies should be able to ensure that admission to systems, repositories, and clouds, and manufacturing environments is precisely controlled and under constant watch and can be proven to be in compliance. Such governance is based on the structural components of Role-Based Access Control (RBAC) and Segregation of Duties (SoD).

In a compliance-oriented DevOps paradigm, access control is not just the matter of allowing entry, but it is the imposition of accountability, avoidance of conflict of interest, creation of valid audit evidence, and facilitation of ongoing regulation. Poorly assigned privileges may compromise the integrity of CI/CD pipelines, leaking sensitive data, and invalid compliance claims may be claimed. Thus, both RBAC and SoD need to be designed in terms of embedded governance controls within the DevOps processes, cloud environments, and automation networks.

This part will look at RBAC and SoD in terms of governance and audit-readiness, their strategic role in creating secure, compliant and scalable delivery environments (Shah, 2024).

4.5.1 Foundations of Role-Based Access Control

Role-Based Access Control is a structured access control model whereby the permissions are given to defined roles and not to individual users. Role membership provides the user with permissions, which allows centralization, ease of governance and streamlined control of policy.

RBAC consists of the following basic elements:

- **Users** – Human actors, service accounts, or automated agents requiring access.
- **Roles** – Logical groupings of permissions aligned with job functions.
- **Permissions** – Authorized operations on specific resources.
- **Sessions** – Active instances of user-role interaction.

In DevOps environments, RBAC applies across multiple layers:

- Source code repositories
- CI/CD orchestration platforms
- Container registries
- Cloud infrastructure
- Monitoring and logging systems
- Secrets management tools

Rather than granting ad hoc permissions, roles are designed around operational responsibilities such as developer, release engineer, security analyst, platform administrator, or compliance auditor. This abstraction improves the ability to scale and reduces privilege sprawl.

4.5.2 Governance Objectives of RBAC in DevOps

RBAC facilitates a number of governance targets that are essential in creating audit-ready, compliance-based DevOps pipelines. Access control should not just limit who is authorized to do what but also provide a formal governance tool used in high-velocity delivery environments to provide accountability, traceability, and reduction of risks.

- **Enforcement of Least Privilege:** The least privilege principle guarantees that the users, service accounts, and automation agents are granted access to the minimum required to carry out their respective assigned duties. In DevOps setting where infrastructure, code repositories and production systems are closely coupled, over permissions are a major contributor to insider risk and exposure of attack surfaces. RBAC restricts lateral movements in systems and accidental misconfiguration or privilege misuse by establishing granular roles based on job functions. Least privilege needs to be continuously validated, especially when team sizes develop, and the roles change.

- **Accountability and Traceability:** Each operation completed in the CI/CD pipelines, cloud-based systems, or monitoring systems should have a certain identity and role assigned to it. RBAC improves the traceability, as permissions are associated with defined roles and their history of assigning is recorded. This allows the investigative forensic, incident response investigation and audit validation. In cases of auditing to the system logs, the presence of structured role governance shows that the activities were approved, checked and adjusted to the formal access policies.
- **Policy Standardization Across Environments:** The current DevOps practices are carried out in various environments which include development, testing, staging and production. RBAC guarantees that the permission structures are similar across these layers eliminating configuration drift and control inconsistencies. Standardization of roles helps in making access roles less ambiguous and informal delegation of privileges which in most cases arise in environments with rapid changes are prevented.
- **Operational Scalability and Workforce Mobility:** Manual permission management cannot be sustained as organizations grow. RBAC allows onboarding, internal transfers and offboarding to be scaled. Role provisioning is automated, resulting in access change being structured, logged and auditable. **This** scalability is a direct contribution to governance maturity because of decreased administrative error and persistence of unauthorized access.
- **Regulatory Compliance Alignment:** The control of access is one of the basic needs of the global regulatory and control

systems like ISO 27001, SOC 2, PCI DSS, HIPAA, and NIST based standards. RBAC offers written documentation of the fact that access control is officially established, implemented and audited.The definitions of roles can be traced back to particular regulatory clauses and enhance documentation of compliance and audit defensibility.

RBAC cannot be fixed in the continuous governance setting. Role recertification, access review, auto monitoring and exception tracking must be done regularly to make sure that governance objectives are kept in line with the changing risk landscapes.

4.5.3 Designing Effective Role Models in CI/CD Environments

Role Engineering and governance design must be done intentionally in order to achieve an effective RBAC implementation. Weak hierarchies of roles may lead to privilege concentration, complexity proliferation, and compliance weakness.

- **Alignment with Organizational Responsibilities:** Roles should be based on actual job function as opposed to random technical compositions. An instance like a developer position must be assigned to development duties whereas release managers or operative engineer must have distinctly different permissions. This congruence makes access privileges congruent with accountability structures in the organization.
- **Environment-Based Segmentation:** Development, testing, staging, and production environments have varying risks. These distinctions need to be represented by role models. In the non-production environment, developers can be assigned higher privileges whereas in production systems, they can be limited. This type of segmentation minimizes the threat of unauthorized modification of live systems.
- **Separation Between Code Authority and Infrastructure Authority:** The developers can use automated pipelines to provision infrastructure in an Infrastructure-as-Code environment. Nonetheless, governance controls should make sure that the authority to providing infrastructure does not

automatically transfer to unlimited cloud administrative privileges. There are clear demarcations between application development and infrastructure governance which minimize systemic risk.

- **Time-Bound and Conditional Access Controls:** Privileges awarded on a temporary basis due to troubleshooting, emergency repair, or a migration process will have to expire. Time limited access **minimizes** the chances of remaining privileges that can be used later.
- **Service Account Governance:** Automation tools, CI/CD agents and integration services are often run under non-human identities. Such service accounts need to conform to the least privilege principles, including the credential rotation, tracking of activity, and a defined purpose.

In practice, role separation, which is structured, may involve:

- Developers who commit and make contributions of code but cannot give approval of production deployments.
- Relevance engineers that control pipeline coordination, but leave application source code unchanged.
- Security analysts that look into vulnerability scans and audit logs and do not modify system configurations.

Production operators carrying out deployment workflows indirectly using the repository.

This system of organized differentiation contributes to the internal control systems and makes audits more defensible by showing that it was designed with a purpose.

4.5.4 Segregation of Duties in Continuous Delivery

Segregation of Duties (SoD) is a governance principle that mandates that the critical responsibilities among two or more persons are divided to avert fraud, conflict of interest or operational error. Within the traditional IT setting, SoD was implemented by means of hand-approved approvals and documented procedures. In the DevOps systems, where automation helps to expedite deployment processes, SoD needs to be directly integrated into digital workflows.

- **Code Author vs. Code Approver:** The developer is not supposed to make or commit his/her changes to secured branches. The mechanisms of peer review and enforced approval policies guarantee the independent verification of code integrity.
- **Infrastructure Provisioning vs. Security Exception Approval:** Provisioning engineers of the cloud resources should not authorize simulatively grant of deviation of the security baselines. External checks minimize the chances of insecure configurations going into production.
- **Access Granting vs. Access Certification:** The assigners of access roles should not be the same ones that do periodic access recertification. Such segregation ensures the lack of unilateral privilege build up.
- **Pipeline Configuration vs. Deployment Authorization:** The design of the automation pipelines should not be the only authority that issues production releases. Independent release validation is used to check the adherence to change governance standards.
- **Emergency Change Execution vs. Post-Change Review:** Rescuers should not legitimize their corrective measures. The integrity of governance is maintained by independent post-incident review.

Approval gates, conditional workflow logic, branch protection rules, and policy-as-code frameworks can create SoD as part of the automation platform. Integrating SoD into the CI/CD pipelines will have governance persistence even in a high-frequency deployment environment.

4.5.5 Static and Dynamic Separation of Duties

Segregation of Duties can either be used in a static manner or can be dynamic.

- **Static Separation of Duties (SSoD):** The structural prevention of assigning conflicting roles to the same person is provided. As an illustration, a user cannot have two roles of a developer and a production approver at the same point. The model minimizes the risk of inherent conflicts but can restrict flexibility in smaller teams.
- **Dynamic Separation of Duties (DSoD):** It allows a user to be in various roles but not do conflicting actions in the same workflow instance. Automated pipelines impose conditional checks, which prevent forbidden combinations of actions. In this model, there is operational agility, but control integrity is maintained.

These two strategies assist in meeting the internal control systems and governance systems. The decision to use the astatic model or dynamic model is determined by the size of the organization, its riskiness and its complexity of operations.

4.5.6 RBAC as an Audit Evidence Generator

RBAC is preventative as well as providing verifiable audit evidence. Formal access management creates auditable records, which are used in compliance measurements.

The artifacts created by the use of RBAC systems include:

- Records and approval documentation of role assignment.
- Access request and approval logs
- Privileged activity monitoring logs.
- Access recertification reports
- Historical revocation records
- Documentation of exception and override.

Since the DevOps pipeline is a continuous process, it means that the monitoring should also be a continuous process. The centralized logging systems consolidate the data on access activity, and, through this, the auditors can assess the success of controls without interrupting the routine activities.

The process of automated extraction of evidence in identity governance systems will make the audits more efficient, fewer people will be engaged in manual documentation, and the level of reliability will be more reliable.

4.5.7 Centralized Identity and Access Governance

Contemporary DevOps ecosystems encompass cloud environments, SaaS environments, container orchestration systems, and monitoring environments. RBAC can also not do without centralized identity governance systems.

Key components include:

- Single sign-on identity providers.
- Multi-factor authentication enforcement.
- Privileged access management solutions.
- Automated deprovisioning and provisioning.
- Periodic recertification campaigns of access in the case of access.

Centralization will offer uniformity and minimize configuration drift amongst systems. Nonetheless, centralization also comes with the concentration of risk; identity systems will become key resources that will need a higher level of protection, encryption, and surveillance.

4.5.8 Risks and Pitfalls in RBAC Implementation

Although RBAC enhances governance, its bad deployment can open fresh vulnerabilities.

Common challenges include:

- **Role Explosion** – Proliferated granular roles generate complexity in the management.
- **Privilege Creep**- Privileges are not revoked as the user gains more and more permissions.
- **Shadow Access** - Temporary permission is made permanent.

- **Excessive Automation with no Governance**- Automated provisioning without governing.
- **Inadequate Documentation** - Weak Documentation Role definitions were not documented or aligned to risk assessments.

To curb these risks, there should be the continuous review and governance maturity checks.

4.5.9 RBAC and Zero Trust Architecture

RBAC is consistent with the principles of Zero Trust security, which presuppose the absence of implicit trust according to the location in the network or prior authentication.

Zero Trust integration incorporates:

- Ongoing identity verification.
- Context-based access controls.
- Device posture validation
- Privilege of just-in-time.
- Ongoing observations of privileged sessions.

Embedded into DevOps, Zero Trust principles help to make sure that the integrity of a pipeline is secured in both distributed or remote working environments.

4.5.10 Strategic Role of RBAC and SoD in Continuous Governance

RBAC and SoD in the context of compliance-based DevOps are no longer controls that are applied to the system in one step at the beginning of its deployment. They are responsive administrative tools that need:

- Ongoing risk assessment
- Suitability to changing regulatory demands.
- Connectedness with change management processes.

- Continuous monitoring and reporting.
- Periodical internal audit certification.

Mature organizations consider access governance as a dynamic process, incorporated in the general continuous compliance framework.

Role-Based Access Control and Segregation of Duties are not only security features of the technical aspect but are also indicators of maturity of governance in the digital businesses. Companies reporting the inclusion of RBAC and SoD in their CI/CD pipelines, cloud design and automation systems exhibit structural dedication to responsibility, openness, and regulatory austerity.

Access governance is an area of control that can be measured in the context of audit-ready DevOps pipelines. It creates perpetual evidence, puts ethical operational limits, minimizes insider threats, and builds the trust of stakeholders. With the growing regulatory attention and the rising delivery speed, the rigorous use of RBAC and SoD is necessary to maintain secure, compliant, and resilient software delivery ecosystems.

Multiple Choice Questions (MCQs)

1. **What is the primary purpose of logging in a DevOps environment?**

   A. To increase deployment speed

   B. To reduce infrastructure costs

   C. To maintain traceability and support audits

   D. To automate testing

2. **Which of the following tools is commonly used for centralized log management?**

   A. Jenkins

   B. Kubernetes

   C. Splunk

   D. Docker

3. **In Continuous Delivery (CD), audit requirements mainly focus on:**

   A. Manual approvals for every deployment

   B. Automated traceability and compliance validation

   C. Eliminating documentation

   D. Reducing system monitoring

4. **Which practice ensures audit compliance without slowing down DevOps pipelines?**

   A. Skipping documentation

   B. Embedding compliance checks into CI/CD pipelines

   C. Disabling monitoring tools

   D. Avoiding automation

5. **In DevOps, change management is best supported by:**

   A. Informal verbal approvals

   B. Automated workflows with documented approvals

   C. No approval processes

   D. Randomized deployment schedules

6. **Which system is commonly used to track and manage change requests?**

   A. Version control systems

   B. Ticketing systems

   C. Antivirus software

   D. Firewall logs

7. **What is a key benefit of maintaining continuous audit readiness?**
   A. Reduced transparency
   B. Faster audit response and reduced compliance risk
   C. Elimination of monitoring tools
   D. Increased manual processes
8. **During an external audit, which document is most critical?**
   A. Marketing strategy report
   B. Deployment frequency report
   C. Audit trail and evidence logs
   D. Customer satisfaction survey
9. **The main objective of Role-Based Access Control (RBAC) is to:**
   A. Provide unlimited access to developers
   B. Restrict system access based on job roles
   C. Eliminate user authentication
   D. Increase system downtime
10. **Segregation of Duties (SoD) helps prevent:**
   A. Automation
   B. Code reviews
   C. Conflict of interest and fraud risks
   D. Continuous integration

Answers

1	2	3	4	5	6	7	8	9	10
C	C	B	B	B	B	B	C	B	C

Chapter 5

Advanced Practices and Future Trends

5.1 CLOUD-NATIVE COMPLIANCE AND SHARED RESPONSIBILITY MODELS

Organizations have changed their methods for creating and managing digital systems because of the fast growth of cloud-native architectural systems. The use of cloud platforms provides organizations with automatic system scaling capabilities that enable them to develop new products at high speed, but these capabilities also bring about new challenges for meeting regulatory requirements. Compliance frameworks from the past emerged because organizations needed to develop their computing systems within fixed operational zones that their IT departments managed from central locations. Dynamic API-based systems of cloud-native ecosystems use infrastructure components that organizations can build, manage, and use through automated systems which operate in shared workspace environments. DevOps pipelines that require compliance need to develop new governance methods to manage this fundamental change in operational practices. Cloud-native compliance has evolved into a continuous automated system which organizations implement at every architectural level of their business operations. The shared responsibility model describes how cloud service providers and customers share their duties for meeting compliance requirements, which stands as a fundamental aspect of this process. Organizations need to master this model because it functions as the key to maintaining their auditing process for cloud-based DevOps operation centers (V, 2023).

5.1.1 Understanding Cloud-Native Architecture in the Context of Compliance

The core characteristics of cloud-native systems include their use of microservices architectures and containerization and orchestration platforms, together with Infrastructure-as-Code (IaC) and serverless computing and automated CI/CD pipelines. The technologies enable quick deployment together with system resilience, but they introduce governance problems which include the following issues:

- Infrastructure instances that last only for short periods of time
- The system automatically creates resources without any human intervention
- The system maintains separate logs that track activities across different services
- The system operates in both multi-cloud environments and hybrid-cloud environments
- The system has complicated rules that govern identity and access management

Static documentation and manual verification processes cannot ensure compliance in these types of environments. The system requires controls to be integrated into all aspects of provisioning scripts and container images and orchestration templates and deployment pipelines. The organization needs to establish infrastructure compliance requirements through coding and version control systems, which will be continuously authenticated throughout the process.

The process of cloud-native compliance requires organizations to implement compliance systems from the design phase instead of performing compliance auditing activities after completion of their projects.

5.1.2 The Shared Responsibility Model

The shared responsibility model serves as the fundamental element which establishes all aspects of cloud governance. The model which defines security and compliance management responsibilities between cloud providers and customer organizations maintains its operational framework.

While variations exist across service models (IaaS, PaaS, SaaS), the fundamental principle remains consistent:

- The cloud provider is responsible for security "of" the cloud.
- The customer is responsible for security "in" the cloud.

The provider typically manages:

- Physical data centers
- Hardware infrastructure
- Networking backbone
- Hypervisors and virtualization layers
- Core platform services

The customer organization remains accountable for:

- Data protection and classification
- Identity and access management
- Application security
- Configuration of cloud services
- Network segmentation within virtual environments
- Compliance with regulatory obligations

The regulatory accountability needs to remain with the organization instead of being passed to the cloud provider. Even outsourcing its infrastructure, the organization should not break the laws of data protection and the industry requirements and obligations of its contracts.

5.1.3 Compliance Implications Across Service Models

Responsibilities of compliance also differ with the model of the cloud service:

1. **Infrastructure as a Service (IaaS)**

   Organizations provide control on operating systems and applications and middleware and configuration components. Security threats of a system occur due to misconfigurations comprising of open buckets of storage and ineffective firewall policies and broad permissions. The mechanisms of governance should pay excessive attention to configuration validation and monitoring.

2. **Platform as a Service (PaaS)**

   This puts more of the underlying platform stack under the control of the provider, but the organization still retains control over application logic, data integrity and identity controls. There is a change in compliance focus on secure coding practices and access governance.

3. **Software as a Service (SaaS)**

   The provider operates almost everything in terms of infrastructure and application components. Nonetheless, data, user access, and configuration of integration are still controlled by organizations. The risks may be due to incorrect role assignment, a weak authentication policy, or a lack of monitoring.

These differences are very critical in order to design risk-based compliance controls.

5.1.4 Cloud Misconfiguration and Compliance Drift

Cloud-native environments are very volatile. Changes in infrastructure take place as automated scripts, api and orchestration engines. This speed creates the risk of compliance drift - where implemented configurations creep out of tolerance of endorsed security baselines.

Some of the common causes of compliance drift are: Cloud-native environments are very volatile. Changes in infrastructure take place as automated scripts, api and orchestration engines. This speed creates the risk of compliance drift - where implemented configurations creep out of tolerance of endorsed security baselines.

Some of the common causes of compliance drift are:

- Manual configuration overrides
- Inconsistent Infrastructure-as-Code templates
- Governance controls bypassed in cases of emergencies.
- Poor versioning of deployment scripts.
- Lack of continuous monitoring

To mitigate drift, organizations must implement:

- Policy-as-Code frameworks
- Automated configuration authentication.
- Hacker-type tools: Continuous compliance scanning tools.
- Real-time alerting for deviations
- Immutable infrastructure patterns

Deviations can be identified and rectified before going to production through the direct incorporation of compliance checks into CI/CD pipelines.

5.1.4 Policy-as-Code and Infrastructure-as-Code Governance

The combination of Policy-as-Code (PaC) and Infrastructure-as-Code (IaC) is one of the most radical changes in cloud-native compliance.

Infrastructure-as-Code declaratively provides cloud provisioning. Policy-as-Code is a set of compliance requirements written in machine-readable forms, which can be automatically enforced on deployment.

Some examples of rules of compliance that may be codified are:

- All the storage services should be encrypted.

- The exposure to the public networks should be limited.
- The logging on of all compute instances is necessary.
- Privileged role should require multi-factor authentication.

The implementation of these policies into deployment workflows guarantees that non-compliant infrastructure cannot be deployed. This converts the compliance to reactive inspection to proactive prevention.

5.1.6 Container and Kubernetes Governance

Container orchestration platforms are often used as the foundations of cloud-native architectures. Containers add some more compliance dimensions:

- Image vulnerability scanning
- Secure base image management
- Secrets management
- Pod-level access control
- Network policy enforcement
- Runtime monitoring

Both build-time and runtime risks have to be covered by compliance controls. Automated scanning tools may be used to validate the images of containers prior to deployment, and runtime policies impose isolation and access limitations.

The containerized environment needs to be governed through integration of the DevOps teams and security governance functionalities to provide consistent enforcement.

5.1.7 Continuous Evidence Collection in Cloud Environments

The conventional audit procedures were based on processed list of documentation and periodical evaluation. Cloud-native systems, on the other hand, generate significant amounts of telemetry and configuration data which can be used as the continuous audit evidence.

The important sources of automated evidence are: The conventional audit procedures were based on processed list of documentation and periodical evaluation. Cloud-native systems, on the other hand, generate significant amounts of telemetry and configuration data which can be used as the continuous audit evidence.

The important sources of automated evidence are:

- Cloud activity logs
- Configuration state snapshots
- Identity and access management records.
- Deployment pipeline logs
- Vulnerability scanning reports
- Infrastructure change histories

When consolidated into centralized compliance dashboards, this data can be used to see near real-time control effectiveness.

On-going collection of evidence maximizes the transparency, cuts down the audit preparation load, and helps in forward-looking remediation.

5.1.8 Multi-Cloud and Hybrid Cloud Governance Challenges

A large number of companies work with different cloud providers and premises. Multi-cloud strategies are more resilient and flexible but make compliance governance more difficult.

Challenges include:

- Lack of uniform policy enforcement measures.
- Varying logging formats
- Dissenting identity management systems.
- Various shared responsibility levels.
- Complex cross-cloud integrations

To address these challenges, organizations must implement:

- Centralized identity federation
- Cross-cloud policy orchestration
- Unified monitoring dashboards
- Standardized compliance baselines
- Governance abstraction layers

This may result in audit preparation fragmentation without the integration of governance architecture.

5.1.9 Risk-Based Cloud Compliance Strategy

The risk assessment should direct cloud-native compliance as opposed to checkbox compliance. Risk based strategies give concern to controls which are founded on:

- Data sensitivity
- Regulatory exposure
- Business criticality
- Threat landscape
- Operational dependencies

This will guarantee the effective distribution of resources in governance and decrease compliance fatigue. Risk management structures need to be incorporated as part of the DevOps processes in organizations so that both security and compliance decisions are in line with the enterprise goals.

5.1.10 Strategic Implications of the Shared Responsibility Model

The shared responsibility model essentially reinvents the organizational responsibility. Instead of contracting the compliance control to infrastructure providers, companies need to develop internal cloud governance functions.

The strategic implications are:

- Building of cloud governance skills.

- Collocation of legal, risk, and DevOps teams.

The second point is an investment in automated compliance tooling.

- Ongoing training of cloud threats.
- Cloud compliance oversight at the executive level.

Established organizations have made cloud compliance an architectural science, and not a reactionary audit mandate.

Cloud-native compliance is a paradigm shift as opposed to static control verification to continuous, automated governance within digital infrastructure. The shared responsibility model does not lessen the regulatory requirements in the organizations, even though it helps in the clarification of the boundaries of accountability. Rather, it requires a higher level of technical maturity, architecture prospect, and integration of governance.

Cloud-native governance in compliance-driven DevOps ecosystems should be proactive, automated and risk-aligned. Continuous monitoring, evidence automation and the creation of Policy-as-Code turn compliance into the bottleneck to be a scale-able innovation enabler. With organizations becoming increasingly dependent on distributed and multi-cloud systems, learning how to make cloud-native compliance not only a technical requirement but a strategic one to maintain audit-compliant, resilient, and future-proof delivery pipelines.

5.2 INTEGRATING DEVSECOPS WITH COMPLIANCE OBJECTIVES

Digital organizations today use DevOps to deliver software more rapidly which changes their entire process for developing and deploying and operating their systems. The absence of governance leads to three issues because organizations face regulatory requirements and encounter operational hazards and deal with complicated auditing processes. Organizations that work in regulated spaces must follow ISO 27001 and SOC 2 and PCI DSS and GDPR and NIST frameworks which means they must integrate compliance requirements from the beginning of their operational processes. Development teams need to create their compliance requirements following the compliance objectives which they will implement throughout their deployment process. The combination establishes DevSecOps which functions as a new operational system that combines security and compliance controls through their development as automated systems, which will undergo permanent testing during the software development lifecycle. DevSecOps improves security systems while changing compliance processes from auditing activities to ongoing governance procedures. Organizations achieve risk reduction and enhanced audit preparation by implementing security engineering methods that match regulatory requirements while measuring their governance development in cloud-based and hybrid computing environments (Ejiofor, 2026).

5.2.1 Evolution from DevOps to DevSecOps

DevOps emerged as a solution to the operational difficulties that resulted from separating development work from operational work. DevOps raised deployment speed through its automated processes and ongoing system integration and delivery practices. Security and compliance requirements were not implemented properly throughout most collaborative systems used in different organizations. The organization used external governance mechanisms which resulted in an operational gap that prevented innovation from being monitored properly.

The system created a governance gap through the existing disconnect. Development teams prioritized fast software delivery while security and compliance teams dedicated their efforts to protecting against risks and following regulations. The absence of integration led to controls being implemented after development work had started which caused organizations to experience operational problems and delays in software release. The regulated industries faced an increased risk of audit findings and control deficiencies because organizations separated their functions and followed inconsistent documentation practices.

The transition to DevSecOps creates a solution for the governance gap because it introduces security and compliance controls into the DevOps pipeline which needs to be followed. Security teams now function as a permanent engineering team instead of serving as a hinderance to the software approval process. The development process includes automated testing together with policy enforcement and configuration validation activities. The system converts compliance from an unexpected requirement to an ongoing process which confirms that all code changes and system builds and deployments meet regulatory standards and risk management protocols.

5.2.2 Shift-Left Security and Regulatory Risk Reduction

Shift-left security requires organizations to include security aspects during the requirements gathering process and the system architecture and design stages. The organization achieves reduced regulatory risk through its practice of implementing security measures from the beginning of its operations. Project teams establish development standards when they create security and compliance requirements during the initial project stage.

Threat modeling operates as the primary structural element of this methodology. Organizations achieve regulatory compliance for confidentiality and integrity and availability controls through their design process, which includes the identification of potential attack paths and sensitive data transfer routes and misuse scenarios. The documentation of threat modeling provides traceable evidence through which risk assessments were performed before implementation, which constitutes an essential requirement for many governance frameworks.

Secure software development life cycle (SDLC) practices support organizations in achieving regulatory compliance requirements. Development processes achieve compliance with software engineering control requirements through the implementation of secure coding standards and design reviews and security checkpoints. Organizations can decrease their remediation expenses and prevent operational disruptions and showcase their governance maturity by addressing security weaknesses and system design problems at an early stage. The implementation of shift-left security helps organizations decrease risks while they establish their security compliance framework.

5.2.3 Automated Security Testing as Continuous Compliance

The development of operations has to be automated to a great extent as automation allows organizations to keep up with their compliance even in fast-changing circumstances. The current manual review process is not able to cope with the greater number of deployments and the rapid changes in the infrastructure. The CI/CD pipelines implement automated security testing to check code and configuration security compliance with established security standards instantly.

Static Application Security Testing (SAST) looks at the source code as it is being written and thus identifies vulnerabilities that can be fixed before the code goes into production. Dynamic Application Security Testing (DAST) evaluates running applications to find security vulnerabilities that can be exploited by attackers when the system operates normally. Software Composition Analysis (SCA) spots third-party library and open-source dependency risks, which ensures that inherited vulnerabilities are detected and resolved.

The automated tools identify technical issues while making structured artifacts that comprise timestamps of their activities.

The results of the scans are stored in the evidence repository, and the remediation tickets and exception approvals and policy assessments are provided, which proves the way the controls work efficiently. The network creates perpetual documentation that reduces the reliance on audit preparation and, at the same time, offers direct visibility. The company applies automated testing as a tool to both regulate its risks and verify its adherence to the law.

5.2.4 Security as Code and Compliance as Code

Cloud-native environments now use code to define both their infrastructure and application configurations. The governance framework extends beyond its existing principles through Security as Code and Compliance as Code. Organizations establish operational consistency through their use of version-controlled scripts which contain policies and control requirements. The Infrastructure as Code (IaC) framework permits organizations to allocate resources automatically while they implement security standards through Their preconfigured security settings. Organizations built infrastructure templates which include access restrictions and encryption settings and network segmentation rules and identity management controls. This solution decreases configuration drift because it requires less manual work to implement changes.

The Policy-as-Code framework provides organizations with a system to implement regulatory compliance through its machine-readable rules which assess deployment activities. The pipeline blocks deployment until necessary fixes take place when a configuration detects a violation of compliance requirements through improper access privileges or unencrypted storage. The preventive model establishes a different approach from traditional detective compliance because it identifies violations after systems start operating. DevSecOps environments achieve compliance risk reduction through their focus on preventive controls which improve governance processes.

5.2.5 Continuous Vulnerability Management and Audit Readiness

Organizations need to maintain ongoing supervision to achieve compliance requirements because it cannot be met through one-time assessment. The process of continuous vulnerability management identifies and resolves newly discovered security threats and existing configuration flaws and dependency vulnerabilities throughout all system stages.

DevSecOps operates under three main components to establish the process of operational workflows that comprise the techniques of vulnerability scanning and prioritization and auto-ticket systems. The models of risk scoring are used to make decisions on priority of remediation depending on its severity and consequences. Service-level goals determine the required time of remediation that is used to hold organizations accountable to their service promises.

On-going vulnerability management demonstrates audit officials that organizations employ proactive ways in which they address their security threats. The operational discipline of the organization manifests itself in the capability to monitor three key areas that comprise the progress of remediation and the past history on the area of vulnerability and patch deployment history. Organizations maintain a current compliance position that provides real performance information that will sustain their audit requirements rather than preparing documentation only when an audit occurs. The process of ongoing readiness development enables organizations to build stakeholder confidence while decreasing their legal risk.

5.2.6 Cultural and Organizational Integration

Sustainable DevSecOps integration requires organizations to change their cultural practices while implementing new technological systems. Development teams and operations teams and security teams need to understand and accept all compliance targets that their work requires. The governance initiatives face the threat of returning to isolated operations when organizations fail to establish shared accountability. Security teams receive protection during project implementation through security frameworks which provide protection during development and discussion of architectural structures and project completion assessments. Security champions who work directly with development teams help organizations implement best practices while creating communication pathways between engineering departments and governance teams.

Developer training programs which teach secure coding and regulatory knowledge and risk management methods enable developers to develop the skills needed to design systems properly. The establishment of performance metrics and quality standards enables organizations to link their compliance objectives with their operational success. Technical controls gain organizational support which enables them to maintain their governance development throughout time.

5.2.7 DevSecOps as a Compliance Enabler

The fundamental function of DevSecOps changes compliance requirements which organizations must meet through this process by creating ongoing capabilities which organizations can use at any time. Organizations achieve successful governance through the implementation of automated validation systems which they use to confirm their delivery pipelines and monitor their operational activities throughout their entire system. The system enables organizations to achieve their goals of implementing quick innovation while they maintain their required regulatory standards.

The traditional audit methods used in dynamic environments which contain cloud and microservices systems that use temporary infrastructure face challenges because their operations keep changing. DevSecOps provides continuous assurance by ensuring that each deployment is evaluated against predefined compliance standards. Executive leadership gains real-time insight into control effectiveness, risk posture, and remediation progress.

DevSecOps serves as a technical framework which enables organizations to accelerate their governance processes. Through this process, organizations achieve operational agility which they need for their business functions while they follow their required regulatory requirements. Organizations need to maintain their security standards through compliance testing processes which measure their achievement of necessary security controls.

The integration of DevSecOps with compliance objectives functions as the successful development of contemporary governance systems. Organizations create a sustainable continuous assurance system through their implementation of preventive controls and automated validation systems and regulatory requirement documentation and cross-departmental responsibility systems. Compliance evolves from a periodic audit-driven exercise into an engineering-driven discipline supported by measurable controls and real-time transparency. The growing digital complexity and stricter regulatory requirements of contemporary systems find their solution through DevSecOps which establishes the organizational framework that enables companies to merge their innovative processes with their obligation to maintain control. Through its activities, the organization improves business resilience while it develops its capability to operate at higher levels of efficiency.

5.3 SCALING COMPLIANCE ACROSS MULTI-TEAM DEVOPS ENVIRONMENTS

With the increase in digital capabilities in organizations, DevOps practices tend to transform into team-based one-off applications to model-like enterprise-wide operations. Several development teams are running simultaneously on a variety of products, platforms and geographical locations in large organizations and quickly expanding mid-sized organizations. Although such scaling increases speed to innovate and responsiveness in the market, it also creates great complexity in governance. The differences in tooling, inconsistent security routines, fragmented documentation, and a decentralized decision-making process might produce some compliance gaps, which are hard to locate and even harder to address (AlZagha, 2025).

Multi-team DevOps environments are also more challenging to scale compliance than technical standardization; they need a deliberate governance architecture. Regulatory demands should be effectively interpreted, converted into executable controls and implemented among the distributed teams without compromising agility. The difficulty is to strike a balance between autonomy and accountability-giving teams the freedom to be creative and at the same time hold them accountable so that the enterprise-wide compliance requirements are met in a consistent manner. In this section, the author focuses his attention on the governance systems, operational frameworks, cultural strategies, and technological mechanisms that are required to scale compliance effectively multi-team DevOps ecosystems.

5.3.1 Governance Architecture for Scaled DevOps

As DevOps grows to cover multiple teams, it can no longer be informal or implicit in its governance. This leads to the need of a structured governance architecture that facilitated the alignment between the enterprise risk management goals and the execution on a team level. Such architecture establishes decision rights, model of accountability, control ownership and mechanisms of policy enforcement.

There are usually three governance models implemented in organizations, which are centralized, federated, and hybrid. In centralized models, compliance standards and control structures are determined and imposed by a central governance role. This will guarantee standardization but can reduce responsiveness. Federated models are those in which compliance responsibility is delegated to the teams at a higher level but the top-level overview is maintained. Hybrid models are implemented decentrally and centrally defined policy with flexibility within established guardrails.

Governance architecture must present a clear explanation of the requirements of any structure in relation to conversion of the requirements into pipeline controls, documentation standards and practices of evidence retention. It has clear escalation routes, exception management processes and acceptance criteria of risks that makes sure that any deviations are not existing but analyzed in a formal way. The absence of this clarity makes scaled DevOps environments prone to be disconnected and not cohesive as far as regulatory compliance is concerned.

5.3.2 Standardization of Controls Across Teams

One of the compliance risks of multi team DevOps is variability. The different teams may possess different CI/CD tools, cloud architecture, security testing processes or documentation processes. The fact is that due to technical diversity, the innovation could be facilitated, yet the issue increases the difficulty in supervising compliance and preparing audits.

When individuals talk of standardization, it does not refer to the same technology but uniformity of the control objectives. The enterprises should define, and all teams implement baseline security and compliance controls regardless of differences in the toolchains. These bases may include mandatory code scan thresholds, encryption options, access policies, log policies, and incident response policies.

Consistent management catalogs provide an equitable point of reference to all the teams. Mapping the enterprise controls to the regulatory clauses will ensure that the distributed groups are conversant with the reasoning behind the requirements. Automated systems of policy enforcement that are performed in pipelines also assist in the standardization process since deviations are suppressed at the implementation level. This style enables groups to be innovative in terms of agreed compliance limits.

5.3.3 Scaling Infrastructure and Policy Enforcement

Due to the spread of DevOps practices, infrastructure must support increased workloads and higher deployment and operation frequency, with operations occurring in more than one location. The organization must have a scalable infrastructure since it is used by both operational requirements and compliance requirements. Compliance with security requirements remains secure due to infrastructures that automatically scale up and down without a fixed security environment.

Infrastructure as Code (IaC) allows standardized environmental provisioning. Standards environments that are formed by the security configurations that organizations incorporate in their code templates are those that are in line with regulatory mandates. Policy-as-Code systems go further to apply this principle by automatically assessing infrastructure and application settings in relation to compliance policies before they are deployed.

The system has a fixed set of standardized limits of operation that every team should abide by at peak workload times until the time of team expansion. Scalable infrastructure and automated policy validation systems are the two important elements in large organizations that promote compliance resilience, as their governance processes are being changed to accommodate the increasing operation in large organizations.

5.3.4 Knowledge-Sharing Frameworks and Documentation Governance

The process of scaling DevOps between different teams requires the knowledge-sharing mechanisms to be structured. In the absence of central documentation and repositories of knowledge, lessons learned, best practices, and interpretations of compliance are kept in silos. Such fragmentation makes the risk of inconsistent implementation and duplication of efforts high.

The creation of a centralized system of knowledge sharing encourages transparency and sameness in operations. Institutional memory is formed through documentation repositories, version-controlled policy libraries, architectural standards, and incident post-mortem records. A clear definition of documentation standards guarantees the consistency of formatting, terms, and control mapping.

The promotion of the input provided by all teams makes the compliance practices collectively owned. Periodical audits of document repositories guarantee that the content is up-to-date and in accordance with a changing regulatory environment. Knowledge-sharing institutionalization helps organizations to lower compliance costs and speed up the onboarding of new teams.

5.3.5 Democratizing DevOps Tools for Compliance Visibility

The process of making DevOps tools usable by all people instead of just development teams will lead to better transparency and cross-team work. All stakeholders, including compliance officers, security analysts, auditors, and business users, need to see deployment pipelines and testing results and risk assessments. The use of shared repositories together with version control systems enables teams to trace code changes and configuration modifications. The dashboarding tools deliver current data about vulnerability patterns, deployment activities, and the status of remediation work. Project information that is easy to access enables teams to work without manual reporting while making compliance decisions based on data. Non-technical users can understand compliance metrics through interfaces that do not require advanced engineering skills. The ability to access information about compliance processes enables technical teams to work with governance teams, which helps them make better decisions based on actual business operations instead of using fixed reports.

5.3.6 Metrics and KPIs for Enterprise Compliance Scaling

The effectiveness of scaled DevOps compliance initiatives needs to be evaluated using measurement. Well-established Key Performance Indicators (KPIs) offer objective work performance indicators that are indicative of governance maturity and operational robustness. Some of the typical measures are deployment frequency, mean time to recovery (MTTR), change lead time, vulnerable remediation schedules, and compliance scan pass rate. Although these metrics are found in the DevOps performance frameworks, they can also be used in compliance goals as they show the reliability of the system, its responsiveness, and effectiveness in control. Team aggregation provides an enterprise-wide perspective of the risk trends and compliance posture. The performance indicators consolidated by the use of executive dashboards assist the leadership in assessing the performance of the governance objectives in terms of consistency. This is a fact-based practice that makes compliance to become the subjective assessment, or more accurately, an operationally measurable practice.

5.3.7 Automation, Monitoring, and Continuous Assurance

Within multi-team environments, automation is the major factor that ensures compliance. It is not scaled to a substantial number of pipelines and rollouts with manual control. Automation of repetitive processes, particularly testing, configuration checking, and documentation, may help reduce the amount of human error and offer a more standardized control application.

Continuous monitoring tools provide proactive detection of abnormalities, configuration changes, and performance degradation. Automated notifications alert the teams of predetermined thresholds that have been violated, and remediation is applied automatically. Audit records of monitoring records and alerts history can be helpful in themselves and can indicate that a continuous control exists.

Organizations will offer ongoing checks and balances through the introduction of automated checks throughout the pipeline. There is compliance validation that is issued each time a code commit, infrastructure update, or deployment is done. Such a proactive model reduces the risks of systemic failures and long-term regulatory alignment.

5.3.8 Incident Management and Operational Resilience

Incidents are bound to occur in scaled DevOps environments. The difference between mature organizations and disruption is that the former are well-organized to respond to it when it occurs, whereas the latter are not. The incident management processes are clearly defined in compliance governance.

The incident identification, classification, escalation, and resolution process should be made uniform among teams. Root cause analysis will ensure that root cause flaws in control are identified and rectified. The lessons learnt have to be documented and placed in knowledge repositories to eliminate repetitions.

There is also enhanced resilience through 24/7 support of operations, whether in-land or external partner. Proactive monitoring and maintenance of the systems also ensures that operational risk is minimized.

Such well-organized activities prove to the regulators and auditors that the organization has controlled discipline even in dynamic and high-volume operations.

5.3.9 Workforce Readiness and Cultural Alignment

Compliance standards require more than technical controls because they need ongoing compliance through organizational governance, which requires workforce readiness. As organizations expand their DevOps footprint, they need to provide their employees with both technical skills and compliance training that enable work in restricted environments.

Organizations need complete training programs that teach staff both technical skills for CI/CD automation and cloud management, and the regulatory requirements that apply to their specific industry. Cross-functional collaboration initiatives enable organizations to break down their operational barriers, which results in shared responsibility for achieving compliance targets.

An organizational culture that supports experimentation, together with ongoing development, creates conditions for businesses to achieve success in the future. Teams use compliance as a tool that helps them integrate their innovative projects with governance requirements. Professional development and open communication from leadership strengthen the cultural connection process throughout the organization.

5.3.10 Change Management in Enterprise DevOps Transformation

The adoption of DevOps practices can be accompanied by a significant change in the organization. The perceived increase in workload, the fear of being replaced, and the feeling of being uncertain about the new processes may lead to resistance. Good change management is thus necessary to reduce the disturbance and create acceptance. Effective expression of strategic goals helps in making the stakeholders aware of the purpose of scaling initiatives. Employee involvement also enhances engagement and lessens resistance since they are involved in the decision-making processes. Pilot implementations enable organizations to work out the practice too much before widespread implementation, which reduces risk and instills confidence.

Change management models focus on incremental adoption, feedback, and continuous improvement. Organizations can be confident that, by integrating compliance considerations in transformation roadmaps, governance objectives can be kept prescriptive during expansion undertakings. One of the most challenging issues of contemporary digital governance is the scaling of compliance in multi-team DevOps settings. The fact that the organization has an increasing ability to provide software increases the likelihood of inconsistent controls and uneven adherence to regulations. The solution to this dilemma needs to be holistic to encompass the governance architecture, uniform structures of control, scalable infrastructures, policy implementation by default, knowledge sharing, performance gauging, workforce development, and structured change management.

When developed correctly, the scaled DevOps compliance transforms the governance into a responsive control mechanism into a distributed and continuously tested responsibility system. This does not impair agility because automation, transparency, and cultural alignment can be used to deliver compliance goals at the team level. Scaling to meet compliance and meet innovation is not only advantageous in a world that is marked by scaling technological innovation and mounting regulatory hurdles, but also a requirement of enterprise sustainability and continuing governance sophistication.

5.4 USING AI AND ANALYTICS FOR COMPLIANCE INSIGHTS

The modern regulatory world is not about compliance as a fixed role that is based on documentation and post-audit audits. It has emerged as an active area that must continually unpuzzle complex demands of control, trace vast functional ecosystems, and respond immediately to quickly emerging threats. Companies nowadays produce huge amounts of data that are of compliance significance- system logs, financial transactions, access logs, assessments of vendors, results of control tests, attestation of policies, and reports of incidents. But nothing can be done with this information without smart processing, which makes it siloed and underutilized. The Artificial Intelligence (AI) and sophisticated analytics convert this piecemeal information into systematic, operational intelligence. (Jonker, 2025).

The implementation of AI in compliance operations is a paradigm shift in the control validation by reactive controls to proactive risk intelligence. The conventional compliance programs are based on manual selection and infrequent reviews, as well as the investigation conducted after the fact. Although these techniques are still significant, they are inadequate when used in a fast digital space. Artificial intelligence helps companies to find non-obvious correlations, detect abuse, anticipate control breakages, and reveal systemic vulnerabilities before they turn into regulatory violations. Organizations can pose the question, what is likely to go wrong, and how can we prevent it? instead of posing the question, what went wrong?

In addition to operational productivity, AI-based compliance analytics increases the strategic importance of the compliance function. It enables risk officers, audit committees, and the executive leadership to visualize trends, quantify exposure, intelligently allocate resources, and align compliance strategy to the overall enterprise risk management objectives. AI can help organizations change their focus on compliance as a liability into compliance as a competitive advantage by converting raw compliance data into proactive knowledge.

5.4.1 Building the Data Architecture for Intelligent Compliance

Compliance based on AI starts with a strong data architecture. The information related to compliance is usually spread over several systems - government, risk and compliance (GRC) platforms, IT service management tools, enterprise resource planning systems, human resource databases, security monitoring tools, and third-party risk management solutions. The databases are represented in various forms, names, and control identifiers. In the absence of harmonization, analytics initiatives will be haphazard and unreliable.

Coherent compliance data architecture comprises aggregation of information in centralized data, normalization, tagging of metadata, and regulatory mapping. Findings of the controls should be related to risk, business line, asset types, and regulatory requirements. Data lineage tracking provides the ability to determine the origin of data systems through analytical results, and this is crucial whenever regulatory entities perform audits. The system should have data quality management practices, i.e., validation checks, duplicate detection, and standardized taxonomies.

Moreover, organizations should adopt safe data governance systems to achieve privacy, confidentiality, and ethical use of information. Retention policies, encryption mechanisms, and access controls are crucial. AI systems can only be as good as the input they consume; thus, the initial requirement of useful compliance insights is developing an integrated, quality database.

5.4.2 Descriptive and Diagnostic Analytics: Understanding the Present

The initial level of AI-based compliance analytics deals with a descriptive and diagnostic level. Descriptive analytics provides a concise yet clear picture of the present compliance position of the organization. It measures such indicators as the rate of control effectiveness, median time to be on the remediation cycle, frequency of audit findings, policy attestation completion rate, and accuracy of regulatory reporting.

Diagnostic analytics is more comprehensive and uncovers the causes. By analyzing the consolidated actions across audits and lines of business, AI tools can spot systemic weaknesses, which could be the presence of recurring access control controls in specific units or a recurring due diligence control problem in specific areas. The NLP techniques are capable of extracting information out of narrative audit reports, whistleblower reports, or incident descriptions and recognizing patterns of themes that would not be obvious otherwise.

The step enhances visibility and transparency. Instead of having to compare trends manually, the compliance teams get automated evidence-based explanations as to why certain risks persist. Specific remediation measures would be supported by diagnostic knowledge in comparison with wholesome, resource-consuming remedial measures.

5.4.3 Predictive Analytics: Anticipating Regulatory Risk

Predictive analytics is an important breakthrough in compliance intelligence. Machine learning models can be used to determine the probability of subsequent compliance failure by studying the historical patterns of incidents, audit findings, and control failures. As an example, algorithms can be used to identify that delayed remediation on high-risk systems is often the precursor to data breaches, or that fraud risks are associated with certain behavioral patterns.

This prediction model can consider the combined effect of several variables, such as control testing frequency, employee turnover, system access changes, vendor performance metrics, and regulatory changes, creating a risk probability score. These insights enable organizations to focus on the priorities of monitoring and distribute assets to the most exposed areas.

Notably, predictive analytics does not usurp human management. Rather, it improves professional judgment because it gives probabilistic estimates. These forecasts enable compliance leaders to enhance controls beforehand, undertake specific control training, or present emergent risks to executive committees before it becomes a reportable violation.

5.4.4 Prescriptive Analytics: Guiding Decision-Making

Prescriptive analytics lifts the prediction capabilities by prescribing measures. AI systems can suggest the most optimal course of action to take, rather than simply identifying the regions that are at risk. As an illustration, the control weakness in a business unit may be recommended to be tested more frequently, access controls revised, or segregation-of-duty imposed more by the system.

The optimization algorithms can be simulated to implement different remediation strategies and evaluate the impact on the reduction of risk and cost-efficiency. Scenario planning helps companies to identify how compliance will be exposed to changes in regulation, expansion of operations, or technology migration. The decision-support tools will enable the compliance leaders to be strategic in their operations instead of being reactive.

Prescriptive insights are to be reviewed by the compliance professionals at all times to ensure that the context is suitable. The AI recommendations are not a set of instructions, but decision facilitators. This is an anthropocentric method of accountability and ethical responsibility.

5.4.6 Real-Time Monitoring and Continuous Compliance

One of the most radical applications of AI in compliance is real-time monitoring. The more traditional compliance tests tend to be periodic and tend to be sample-based. This would lead to gaps in between review cycles where the failures in control could go undetected. Nevertheless, AI systems can read real-time data feeds at any moment - financial transactions, system access data, communications metadata, and policy compliance measurements.

Anomaly detection algorithms identify deviation of behavior in relation to predetermined behavioral norms. An example is that of suspicious transaction patterns, unauthorized privilege escalation, or abnormality that is associated with vendor payment that can be signaled immediately. Constant surveillance implies that there is less time between the risks taking place and the exposure to the regulatory forces; thus, there is less regulatory and negative publicity.

Besides, there are continuous compliance models that suggest dynamic risk scoring. The linking of new data in the system will automatically rate the risks and provide a close real-time picture of compliance posture in the organization. Such flexibility is particularly relevant to those spheres that are most regulated, e.g., financial services, healthcare, and data-driven companies.

5.4.6 AI in Regulatory Change Management

The regulatory environments are continuously evolving, and there is a continuous issue of new rules, amendments, and guidance documents in various jurisdictions. The AI-assisted tools can scan regulatory books and periodicals, scan textual requirements, and match them with the existing control frameworks. The natural language processing will assist in defining the applicable themes of the regulations, besides identifying the gaps between the new requirements and the current controls.

Horizon scanning is also automated, and this reduces the chances of stagnated compliance updates. AI-driven mapping tools could suggest the policies to be updated, the controls that require enhancement, and the training programs that are to be optimized further. This not only assists in accelerating the process of reacting to the regulations but also in responding to the dynamism of the legal environment.

5.4.7 Enhancing Audit and Investigation Processes

The internal audit process and investigation process benefit from AI technology, which increases their operational efficiency. The automated evidence collection systems have the capability to collect both system logs, access logs, and transaction records, which they will use for their audit assessments. Text analytics identifies two types of errors in documentation, which include irregularities and unexpected wording patterns found in financial reports. The fraud detection process uses machine learning algorithms to identify specific patterns that appear across extensive datasets.

AI technology enables investigators to create event sequence timelines by linking system logs with communication records and user activity data. The system improves forensic investigation accuracy while also shortening the time needed to complete the investigation process. The compliance professionals use automated systems to do repetitive data analysis work, which lets them concentrate on work that requires their professional judgment and on monitoring activities.

5.4.8 Governance, Ethics, and Model Oversight

The use of AI in compliance functions creates new governance requirements for organizations. The organizations should accomplish three objectives where their AI systems should operate with transparency, fairness, and legal defensibility. Model documentation, validation testing, and performance monitoring are also necessary components in the process. The algorithms should be accompanied by bias detection algorithms that will ensure that they do not generate discriminatory conclusions and unreasonable risk judgments.

The organization should also make data privacy issues as important as other priorities. The AI systems process sensitive data that includes information pertaining to employees and customers and their transactions. The companies should set access control and encryption systems and retention policies to adhere to data protection policies. Both credibility and regulatory trust will be improved through the regular model audit and independent validation review.

Artificial intelligence cannot perform the role of human responsibility, but rather complements it. The ultimate compliance decisions that involve the decision on regulatory reporting and disciplinary action should not be left under the control of human beings. It will ensure that the process is ethically monitored and that the trust of the stakeholders in the automated systems is established.

4.5.9 Measuring Impact and Continuous Improvement

The compliance implementation of AI analytics should be linked to the measurable performance indicators. The organizations can follow some of the measures, some of which are the reduction of audit findings, less remediation time, a greater rate of control effectiveness, and less time to detect anomalies. Subsequent follow-ups of such outcomes indicate the payback and justify AI project success.

Continuous model refinement should also be done. As regulating needs emerge and the operational environment changes, the AI models need to be retrained with the new datasets. The communication between the compliance teams and the data scientists will ensure that the relevance of analytical tools, their accuracy, and their alignment with organizational goals are upheld.

An essential change to the regulatory risk management concerns compliance intelligence with AI and analytics. With an enhanced database, application of layered analytical models, enabling real-time monitoring, and applying governance controls, organizations can turn compliance into a responsive need to a predictive and strategic process.

The use of AI helps compliance units to predict risks, make wise resource usage, and enhance resilience in more complicated regulatory contexts.

Nonetheless, AI does not truly increase compliance because of its automation, but rather its combination with professional expertise. With technological innovation, ethical control, and strategic leadership, compliance is not only an obligation to pass through the audit of regulators, but a formidable driver of responsible and sustainable enterprise development.

5.5 FUTURE OF COMPLIANCE-DRIVEN DEVOPS PIPELINES

The history of DevOps has completely changed the manner in which organizations develop, test, and deploy software. The movement that started in an attempt to speed up the development process and increase inter-team cooperation has grown into a blueprint of enterprise agility. However, with the growing data intensity of digital systems and the escalating regulatory scrutiny of them, DevOps is no longer enough. The compliance-based DevOps pipelines are the future - the delivery ecosystems, in which the governance, risk management, and regulatory enforcement are not added as controls at the lifecycle tail end, but integrated directly into automated processes(Mahoney, 2025).

Compliance will not be viewed as a limit to innovation in the next several years, but rather as a design concept of digital architecture. The scope and complexity of regulatory requirements that pertain to information protection, cybersecurity, artificial intelligence, financial transparency, and information flows across borders are increasing. Those organizations that consider compliance as a frivolous thing will find it difficult to keep up. In comparison, however, those that design pipelines with the capacity to impose policy dynamically, authenticate controls dynamically, and respond to changes in regulation very quickly will benefit strategically.

Intelligence, maturity of automation, predictive governance, and adaptable control models will define the future of compliance-driven DevOps pipelines. These pipes will not only audit policy violations, but they will proactively predict risks, provide corrective measures, and match compliance measures to enterprise performance measures. As the technology and regulation are shifting equally fast, the structural pillar of sustainable digital transformation will become compliance-based DevOps.

5.5.1 From DevOps to DevSecOps to DevRegOps

The advanced stage of DevOps to DevSecOps has been the implementation of security controls into the continuous delivery processes. Its next step, which can be imagined in the form of DevRegOps or Compliance-as-Code ecosystems, takes this integration to regulatory governance. On this model, regulatory requirements are written into machine-readable policies that are embedded inside CI/CD pipelines.

The pipelines of the future will authenticate: Data residency constraints before deployment

- Encryption and key management standards
- Segregation-of-duties configurations
- AI model transparency documentation

- Logging and audit trail completeness

Regulatory controls will operate similarly to automated unit tests: if a change violates a compliance policy, deployment will halt. This automation demands that regulatory validation be done at the pace of the development iterations. The very pipeline itself emerges as a compliance enforcement engine, eliminating the need to conduct reviews manually and speeding up regulatory compliance.

5.5.2 AI-Augmented Compliance Pipelines

The artificial intelligence will become prominent in the next-generation DevOps environments that are based on compliance. Instead of employing a set of rules, AI systems will examine the activity on pipes, identify anomalies, and adjust control thresholds in real-time.

Future capabilities can be:

- Predictive risk scoring for code changes
- Automated identification of regulatory impact across jurisdictions
- Intelligent mapping of new regulations to existing control libraries
- Behavioral anomaly detection within deployment patterns
- Context-aware compliance validation based on asset sensitivity

AI-enhanced pipelines will move beyond static rule enforcement toward adaptive governance. As an example, Deployments with high risks and sensitive data can cause an increase in validation processes, whereas low-risk changes can be handled with a series of simplified checks. This compliance model is agile and regulatively prudent.

5.5.3 Continuous Regulatory Intelligence Integration

The regulatory framework for cybersecurity, artificial intelligence ethics, digital finance, environmental reporting, and consumer data rights protection continues to change because new requirements take effect. Future DevOps pipelines will use automated regulatory intelligence systems, which will update their policy-as-code libraries with real-time data.

Natural language processing systems will scan regulatory publications, interpret key requirements, and suggest modifications to compliance controls embedded in pipelines. Governance teams will review and approve updates before enforcement. The semi-automated process for regulatory synchronization will decrease the time required to implement operational changes when regulations change.

Organizations achieve compliance continuity through their ability to adapt to changing legal requirements. The pipeline functions as both a delivery system and a mechanism for responding to regulatory requirements.

5.5.4 Zero-Trust and Fine-Grained Governance Models

The upcoming compliance-driven pipeline will establish its security framework according to zero-trust architectural principles. The system will continuously authenticate, authorize, and log all deployment actions, access requests, and infrastructure changes. The pipeline automation will incorporate identity-based access controls, which will stop unauthorized changes to schemas and system configurations from occurring.

Organizations will use fine-grained governance models to implement dynamic access policies that assess users based on their current context instead of using broad role-based permissions. The system enables organizations to provide temporary elevated access rights through automated workflows, which will automatically remove these rights after deployment ends. Ephemeral authorization models will help organizations decrease their risk exposure while creating stronger systems for defending audit processes.

The combination of zero-trust principles with compliance automation enables pipelines to defend against both insider threats and credential theft.

5.5.5 Infrastructure-as-Code and Immutable Compliance

The implementation of Infrastructure-as-Code (IaC) practices will enhance the compliance requirements of DevOps pipelines. Through declarative infrastructure configuration definitions, organizations can maintain version control over all system elements, which include application and database updates, network design, cloud access, and security mechanisms. The use of immutable infrastructure models allows organizations to achieve compliance validation through system replacement instead of system changes. Organizations verify their compliance through standardized templates, which they test before their actual deployment. The deployed environments automatically obtain compliance status when the templates meet compliance standards. Future pipelines will incorporate compliance scanning tools, which will assess IaC templates against regulatory requirements before any provisioning occurs. The system prevents the establishment of noncompliant environments through its validation process, which also decreases the need for corrective actions.

5.5.6 Metrics, Transparency, and Board-Level Reporting

The development of compliance-driven DevOps will lead executive leadership to request measurable metrics that assess the effectiveness of pipeline governance. The current compliance reporting system documents incidents together with audit results, but upcoming systems will focus on tracking preliminary signs of compliance. The primary indicators for assessment will include the following metrics:

- Percentage of deployments passing automated compliance checks
- Time required to update policy-as-code after regulatory change
- Frequency of compliance-related pipeline failures
- Reduction in post-deployment remediation incidents
- Risk-adjusted deployment velocity

These metrics enable boards and risk committees to evaluate compliance maturity quantitatively. The transparency dashboards will convert technical pipeline operations into business risk assessments, which will enhance governance control and help in developing organizational strategies.

5.5.7 Ethical AI and Responsible Automation Governance

As automation develops more intelligent systems, the need for ethical supervision will become more crucial. AI compliance systems need to function with transparent operations that eliminate biases while providing understandable results. Organizations must now demonstrate their automated decision-making systems because regulatory bodies require them to do so when customer rights and financial transactions are involved. The upcoming compliance-driven pipelines will include the following elements:

- Model validation checkpoints
- Explainability documentation generation
- Audit logs for AI-based enforcement decisions
- Human-in-the-loop escalation mechanisms

The safeguards work to protect automation, which creates compliance benefits because it creates non-discriminatory automated systems that maintain their accountability requirements.

5.5.8 Convergence with Enterprise Risk Management

The implementation of compliance-based DevOps pipelines will establish strong links to Enterprise Risk Management systems, which will enable organizations to connect their IT functions with their business governance processes. The traditional ERM activities use periodic assessments together with audit findings and management evaluations to update risk registers. The DevOps pipelines operate continuously, which enables them to deliver immediate updates about control checks, deployment results, policy violations, and their associated resolution activities. The operational indicators from these pipelines and ERM platforms will enable real-time updates to risk registers, which will occur without needing to conduct risk assessments after the fact. The transformation establishes risk management as an ongoing reporting mechanism that functions as a dynamic process.

The current method establishes an efficient way to transform DevOps pipelines into tools for detecting strategic risks. The automated compliance checks, which fail to validate requirements together with access control exceptions and configuration anomalies, create additional data points that the organization uses to build its risk profile. The aggregated pipeline data reveals systemic weaknesses because it shows the patterns of policy breaches, slow remediation processes, and excessive override approvals, which indicate future incidents, although they have not yet occurred. The enterprise dashboards should integrate this intelligence because it enables leadership to identify emerging vulnerabilities and decide on their mitigation and approach their risk indicators according to their predefined risk appetite.

The combination of compliance-based pipelines with ERM systems delivers organizational resilience improvements that support better strategic execution. Leadership obtains close real-time visibility of the impacts of digital transformation initiatives concerning regulatory exposure, operational stability, and financial risk. Organizations use current compliance knowledge to make decisions about their innovation projects, investment initiatives, and market entry strategies. Organizations need this convergence because it helps them maintain their operational agility while achieving their governance needs through a unified, data-driven system that supports both innovation and risk management.

The advancement of compliance-driven DevOps pipelines relies on four essential elements, which include intelligence, automation, adaptability, and strategic integration. The governance framework must be incorporated into automated processes because digital systems continue to grow and regulatory requirements become more intricate.

The new compliance architecture will be established through the combination of AI risk analytics, infrastructure-as-code validation, automated regulatory intelligence, and zero-trust enforcement models. The evolution of pipelines will transform them from delivery systems into complete governance frameworks, which will identify risks and apply regulations while ensuring compliance with innovation processes. Organizations that embrace this transformation will achieve controlled velocity, which enables them to develop new products at high speed while following established compliance requirements.

Businesses that refuse to implement modern solutions will face two main problems because their operations will slow down and they will lose their competitive advantage. The development of digital agility, together with the need for regulatory accountability, creates a new future for compliance-driven DevOps pipelines, which will serve as the foundation for responsible, sustainable innovation.

Multiple Choice Questions (MCQs)

1. **In a cloud-native environment, who is primarily responsible for securing the underlying physical infrastructure?**

   A. Customer organization

   B. DevOps team

   C. Cloud Service Provider

   D. Compliance auditor

2. **In the shared responsibility model, customers are typically responsible for:**

   A. Physical data center security

   B. Application security and data protection

   C. Network backbone infrastructure

   D. Hardware maintenance

3. **What is the primary objective of integrating DevSecOps with compliance?**

   A. Eliminate DevOps practices

   B. Delay releases for security reviews

   C. Embed security and compliance into the CI/CD pipeline

   D. Increase manual auditing

4. **Which practice best supports compliance in DevSecOps environments?**

   A. Manual vulnerability scanning after deployment

   B. Continuous monitoring and automated policy enforcement

   C. Ignoring minor compliance violations

   D. Isolating security from development teams

5. **When scaling compliance across multiple DevOps teams, the most effective approach is:**

   A. Centralized manual approval for every deployment

   B. Standardized compliance-as-code frameworks

   C. Independent compliance rules per team

   D. Eliminating compliance documentation

6. **What is a key challenge in multi-team DevOps compliance management?**

   A. Lack of automation tools

   B. Inconsistent policy implementation

   C. Excessive cloud storage

   D. Too few deployment pipelines

7. **How can AI contribute to compliance management in DevOps pipelines?**

   A. Replacing all security professionals

   B. Predicting potential compliance risks using analytics

   C. Eliminating regulatory requirements

   D. Slowing down deployments

8. **Which of the following best describes analytics-driven compliance insights?**

    A. Reactive incident response

    B. Data-driven identification of policy violations and trends

    C. Manual compliance reporting

    D. One-time security audits

9. **The future of compliance-driven DevOps pipelines is likely to focus on:**

    A. Reduced automation

    B. Fully manual governance

    C. Intelligent automation and real-time compliance validation

    D. Eliminating compliance checks

10. **What role does compliance-as-code play in modern DevOps practices?**

    A. Increases paperwork

    B. Automates policy enforcement within pipelines

    C. Replaces CI/CD tools

    D. Reduces collaboration

Answers

1	2	3	4	5	6	7	8	9	10
C	B	C	B	B	B	B	B	C	B

Bibliography

AlZagha, R. (2025). *Simplifying Authorization at Scale: The Importance of DevOps Workflows with Flexible, Scalable and Secure Access Control.*

Bigham, T. (2022). *DevRiskOps: Risk management in DevOps.*

Bugle, A. S. (2023). *How to Build An Automation Governance Framework For Your Low-Code AI.*

Chase, T. (2025). *Securing Your Source Code: A Critical Defense Against Modern Threats.*

Ejiofor, J. (2026). *Secure DevOps at Scale: Integrating SRE, DevSecOps and Compliance.*

Faghihi, F. (2025). *15 Essential Regulatory and Security Compliance Frameworks & Industry Standards.*

Heusser, M. (2024). *Rapid release cycles need not compromise the security of an application and supporting infrastructure. Follow these guidelines to ensure security throughout the CI/CD pipeline.*

Holdsworth, J. (2025). *What is secrets management?* https://www.ibm.com/think/topics/secrets-management

Holdsworth, J., & Badman, A. (2025). *What is Infrastructure as Code (IaC)?* https://www.ibm.com/think/topics/infrastructure-as-code

Hollowell, T. (2023). *5 Steps to Improve Your Software Artifact Traceability.*

Jain, R. (2024). *The Six Biggest Challenges of Traditional Audit Techniques.*

Jonker, A. (2025). *AI compliance: What it is, why it matters and how to get started.*

Mahoney, D. (2025). *What Does the Future of Compliance in a CI/CD Pipeline Look Like?*

Mainville, D. (2023). *Change Management Best Practices.*

McCarty, B. (2024). *Author: Becky McCarty | (Partner | CPA, CISA, CRISC, CIA, CFE) Contact Auditor Internal vs External Audit: What You Need To Know.*

Natarajan, M. (2025). *Building Audit-Ready Automation: A Complete Guide.*

Nduhiu, J. (2025). *Common DevOps Roles and Responsibilities Today: Who's on a DevOps Team & How These Roles Work Together.*

Queen, C. (2025). *Policy As Code (PaC).* CrowdStrike. https://www.crowdstrike.com/en-us/cybersecurity-101/cloud-security/policy-as-code/

R, N. (2025). *What Is Continuous Compliance Monitoring? - Key Components & Challenges.* https://www.atlassystems.com/blog/continuous-compliance-monitoring

Shah, N. (2024). *What is Roles-Based Access Control (RBAC)?*

Singirikonda, E. K. (2025). *The Evolution of DevOps: Trends Shaping the Future.*

Taneja, R. (2024). *What is Log Monitoring? Complete Guide for 2026.*

Timar, A. (2026). *Compliance-First: Building Prospecting Workflows That Stay on the Right Side of Platform Rules.*

V, A. (2023). *Shared responsibility model explained: Clear roles & best practices.*

Walker, J. (2025). *Drift Management in Cloud Infrastructure: Best Practices.* Spacelift. https://spacelift.io/blog/drift-management

ABOUT THE AUTHORS

Mahendar Ramidi is a Mobile and Cloud Architect with over 12 years of experience designing secure, scalable, and compliance-driven digital platforms for healthcare, government, and regulated enterprise environments. He specializes in building audit-ready delivery pipelines that integrate DevOps automation, cloud-native infrastructure, and strong governance frameworks.

Mahendar has applied for four patents and authored more than 15 peer-reviewed publications with over 100 scholarly citations, contributing to research in secure mobile architectures, regulated CI/CD systems, intelligent runtime orchestration, and automated auditability. His work focuses on embedding compliance directly into engineering workflows through policy-as-code, encrypted artifact management, traceable build systems, and identity-bound release controls.

In mobile development, he integrates Artificial Intelligence to enhance biometric identity validation, fraud detection, intelligent workflow automation, and decision-support systems within regulated applications. His architectural approach emphasizes privacy-by-design, encrypted local persistence, conflict-aware synchronization, and resilient offline-first models for mission-critical mobile platforms.

Throughout his career, he has led the design of HIPAA-compliant healthcare applications, government digital service platforms, and secure cloud-integrated mobile ecosystems built for transparency and accountability.

Through his research, patents, and architectural leadership, Mahendar advances compliance-driven engineering while shaping the future of secure, AI-enabled mobile systems.

Prudhvi Raju Mudunuri is an enterprise systems infrastructure specialist with extensive experience designing secure, scalable, and compliance-driven digital platforms for regulated enterprise and public-sector environments. He specializes in building automation-centric infrastructure and DevOps ecosystems that integrate security, governance, and auditability as foundational system capabilities. His work focuses on enabling organizations to modernize complex enterprise systems while meeting stringent regulatory, security, and operational requirements.

Prudhvi works at Guidehouse Inc., where he contributes to the design and governance of large-scale, policy-driven enterprise platforms. As a federal contractor, he has supported mission-critical platforms for the National Library of Medicine (NLM) at the National Institutes of Health (NIH), helping architect secure, audit-ready systems operating under rigorous compliance mandates. His expertise spans compliance-driven CI/CD pipelines, infrastructure-as-code frameworks, identity-bound release controls, policy-as-code enforcement, and automated governance models for regulated digital environments.

He holds multiple patents related to zero-trust security, identity, and governance fabrics for regulated enterprise platforms and has authored peer-reviewed publications cited by researchers and practitioners. His work emphasizes embedding compliance directly into engineering workflows through automated controls, traceable build and deployment systems, secure artifact management, and continuous auditability.

In addition to his applied engineering work, Prudhvi actively contributes to the professional and research community as an invited keynote speaker, peer reviewer, editorial board member, and session chair for international conferences and journals focused on AI-enabled enterprise systems, security engineering, and compliance-driven infrastructure. Through his technical leadership and innovation, Prudhvi advances the development of resilient, trustworthy enterprise systems where automation, security, and compliance operate in concert.

www.ingramcontent.com/pod-product-compliance
Lightning Source LLC
LaVergne TN
LVHW022212200926
848481LV00006B/1937

* 9 7 9 8 9 0 3 9 2 5 2 5 4 *